Pamela Hansford Johnson

Twayne's English Authors Series

Kinley E. Roby, Editor
Northeastern University

TEAS 291

PAMELA HANSFORD JOHNSON
Photograph by Jerry Bauer
through the courtesy of Lady Snow

Pamela Hansford Johnson

By Ishrat Lindblad

Stockholm University

Twayne Publishers • Boston

823
J683L

Pamela Hansford Johnson
Ishrat Lindblad

Copyright © 1982
Twayne Publishers
A Division of G. K. Hall & Co.
70 Lincoln Street
Boston, Massachusetts 02111

Printed on permanent/durable
acid-free paper and bound in
the United States of America

Book production by Marne B. Sultz
Book design by Barbara Anderson

Library of Congress Cataloging in
Publication Data

Lindblad, Ishrat.

(Twayne's English authors
series; TEAS 291)
  Bibliography: p. 187
  Includes index.
  1. Johnson, Pamela Hansford,
1912–1981
—Criticism and interpretation.
I. Title. II. Series.
PR6019.03938Z77
823'.912   81-6727
ISBN 0-8057-6762-2   AACR2

Contents

About the Author

Ishrat Lindblad was born in 1940 in Lucknow, India. In 1955 she entered Kinnaird College, Lahore, Pakistan. She obtained her Bachelor of Arts degree in Philosophy, Political Science, and English Honors in 1958 and began teaching at Kinnaird College the same year. She enrolled for her Master of Arts in English at Forman Christian College, Lahore, at the same time, and obtained the degree from the University of the Punjab in 1960. She continued to teach at Kinnaird College with a few lectures at Forman Christian until 1962. In 1964 she joined the University of Uppsala for post-graduate studies in English. She obtained her *filosofie licenciat* from Uppsala in 1968 and her *filosofie doktorsexamen* in 1971. She taught English at Uppsala University from autumn 1968 till summer 1976. In July 1976 she obtained the post of "Docent" (Associate Professor) in the Department of English, Stockholm University, where she is currently employed. She has spent one academic year at Darwin College, University of Cambridge, in 1973–74, when she obtained a British Council scholarship to do research at Cambridge. She has written *Creative Evolution and Shaw's Dramatic Art*, 1971, and on Bernard Shaw, Samuel Beckett, John Fowles, Shakespeare and Dickens.

Preface

Pamela Hansford Johnson was an extremely versatile and prolific writer. She tried her hand at every literary genre. Beginning as a poet in 1934 she wrote short stories, plays, essays, literary criticism, radio broadcasts, murder stories, and no less than twenty-seven novels. After the remarkable success of her first novel, *This Bed Thy Centre*, in 1935, her steady output established her reputation as a serious novelist. In the 1940s the publication of what has come to be known as the "Helena" trilogy (*Too Dear for My Possessing, An Avenue of Stone,* and *A Summer to Decide*) quickened general interest in her work, and in the 1950s *An Impossible Marriage* and *The Last Resort* renewed her claim to fame. The publication in 1959 of her widely acclaimed satirical novel *The Unspeakable Skipton* moved Walter Allen to write that "together with *The Last Resort*, which appeared in 1956 and is surely one of the best novels of our time, it shows that there can no longer be excuse for failure to recognise that Miss Hansford Johnson is as good as any novelist writing in this country today."[1]

Many of the outward marks of success have been bestowed upon her work. She was a fellow of the Royal Society of Literature. She received several honorary degrees. Three of her books were Book Society choices and she herself was a member of the Book Society's Committee. Most of her novels were published simultaneously in both Great Britain and America and several of them have been tranlated into a variety of languages including such diverse ones as Russian and Swedish. In spite of this kind of recognition there have been comparatively few studies of her work. The leading British and American weeklies have always devoted a considerable amount of their space to reviewing her books. Her work is included in most surveys of contemporary British novelists, but Isabel Quigly is the only writer so far to have devoted a study to her work. This study was published in 1968 as part of the "Writers and Their Work" series for The British Council and is, of necessity, a rather brief introduction to the novelist. After its publication Pamela Hansford Johnson wrote six more novels, one of which, *The Survival of the Fittest*, is undoubtedly her most ambitious attempt to render the experience of her own generation. A book-length study of her novels is therefore not only justified, it is long overdue.

Even in a book-length study, it is hardly feasible to include all aspects of her many-faceted production. A book of poems, *Symphony for Full Orchestra*, launched her literary career and some of the early novels use imagery and lyrical description that is clearly influenced by her original interest in poetry. Beyond this, however, Pamela Hansford Johnson herself was the first to dismiss the poems as a false start. Of the plays written with C. P. Snow she said "They were written very frivolously by both of us while on our honeymoon, and it would be impossible now to disentangle which of us wrote what. Anyway, they're of little value."[2] One of her plays, *Corinth House*, does not fall into this category and is recognizably the work of the novelist in terms of situation and character. It is, however, an isolated example and does not warrant a full discussion in its own right, because the view it gives of her authorship is similar to the one that can be gained by concentrating only on the novels. It is as a novelist that Pamela Hansford Johnson thought of herself and as a novelist that she will be remembered. Consequently, it is only logical to devote this study to a detailed presentation and analysis of her novels.

Two novels, the murder stories written in collaboration with Gordon Neil Stewart under the pseudonym Nap Lombard, fall outside her usual range and should be regarded as works of entertainment alone. Of her nonfiction the long prose tract, *On Iniquity*, reveals her preoccupation with the problem of evil and the responsibility that society has toward the individual, but it is not directly relevant to her fiction. Her studies of Thomas Wolfe and Ivy Compton-Burnett reveal her admiration for these two authors and her views on fiction will be referred to where relevant. Her extremely successful radio broadcasts (published as *Six Proust Reconstructions*) using characters from Proust and placing them in France at the time of the German occupation reveal her deep understanding of the work of Marcel Proust. The articles that she wrote on Proust also testify to her special admiration for his masterpiece, and he is the one influence that can unquestionably be traced in her interest in the subjects of time and memory in several of her novels. Apart from Proust it is difficult to determine the influence of specific authors on her work. It seems rather as if she were affected more strongly by the fashions current in the 1930s as reflected in the work of Thomas Wolfe, Aldous Huxley, and Dylan Thomas, with the repeated use of counterpoint and stream-of-consciousness techniques. The presence of these influences is discussed in relation to individual novels whenever it is felt to be relevant.

The critical and analytical discussion of the novels has been organized according to principles of chronology subject to considerations of unity on the basis of characters, modified, when considered necessary, by similarities between novels in terms of setting or theme. It is possible to suggest a line in Pamela Hansford Johnson's development from an early interest in the creation of an ambience and the use of a kind of contrapuntal narrative technique; to a brand of social realism where the lives of individuals are set against the background of world events; and finally to a preoccupation with the problems of human relationships told chronologically by a first- or third-person narrator.

The first and third novels, *This Bed Thy Centre* (1935) and *Here Today* (1937), are strikingly similar in that both of them describe life in one of London's seedy suburbs, using parallel plots to give the impression of a community rather than the story of a particular individual. Consequently they are treated together in the chapter that follows the biographical introduction.

World's End (1937) and *The Monument* (1938) both contain the same character, Arnold Brand, although he has a major role in the former novel and an extremely minor role in the latter. The setting in these two novels is bohemia rather than suburbia, for the main characters have literary ambitions and are politically aware.

They belong to the generation that came of age in the 1930s. The shadows of Spain and of the Second World War loom large in these books. *The Survival of the Fittest* (1968) can be said to belong to the same category, even though it was published some thirty years later, and is therefore discussed at the same time as the others in Chapter 3.

Two somewhat disparate early novels are grouped together in Chapter 4. *Girdle of Venus* (1939), which focuses on the life of a lonely woman who tries to earn easy money through fortune-telling, and *The Family Pattern* (1942), which is set in the past and describes the lives of two sisters, one impoverished and the other well established. Both of these are minor novels and neither of them is easily available since they have never been reissued.

The fifth chapter is devoted to an analysis of the "Helena" trilogy, which has already been sufficiently established as a unity to eliminate the need of much prefatory justification. A fourth novel, *Winter's Quarters* (1943), now out of print and extremely hard to come by, poses something of a problem. It is discussed in the same chapter because several of the characters in the trilogy make a brief appearance in it, but its subject matter and narrative method are essentially different from those of the trilogy proper.

Pamela Hansford Johnson's second novel, *Blessed Above Women* (1936), was a noticeable departure from her first novel and the ones that immediately followed it. In *Blessed Above Women* she tries to penetrate the mind of a person in the grip of an obsessive and hopeless passion. Two later novels, *The Trojan Brothers* (1944) and *The Holiday Friend* (1972), are variations on the same theme and all three novels are discussed together in Chapter 6.

The seventh chapter deals with those novels that are concerned with different aspects of a theme which is, in fact, the title of one of them—an impossible marriage. The heroine in *The Philistines* (1949), *Catherine Carter* (1952), and *An Impossible Marriage* (1954) makes a marriage that restricts her development as a human being and reacts against her situation in an effort to lead a fuller life. The loss of a deeply felt love under the pressures of society is the subject of both *The Last Resort* (1957) and *The Humbler*

Creation (1959), which are therefore treated together in the eighth chapter.

The Unspeakable Skipton (1959), *Night and Silence, Who Is Here?*, and *Cork Street, Next to the Hatter*'s have come to be called "The Dorothy Merlin Comedies" because they share some of the same characters even though they are otherwise unrelated. These three are the only purely satirical novels she has written and are therefore discussed as a group in the ninth chapter.

The four novels that remain to be considered, *An Error of Judgement* (1962), *The Honours Board* (1970), *The Good Listener* (1975), and *The Good Husband* (1978), do not readily fall into categories. All four of them reveal the author's enduring interest in human relationships and the latter two clearly belong together since *The Good Husband* is virtually a sequel to *The Good Listener*. For the sake of convenience the four novels are dealt with chronologically in Chapter 10. The appearance in March 1981 of *A Bonfire* came too late for it to be included in this book.

In the writing of such a study the author accrues many debts of gratitude. Among the people to whom I am most eager to acknowledge my debt and convey my grateful thanks is the subject of my study, Lady Pamela Snow, who was extremely generous in replying to letters, granting permission to examine whatever material I have needed, and to interview her myself. Her cooperation has been invaluable and far beyond what I could have hoped for. Her death on June 19, 1981, occurred while this book was in press with the result that I refer to her throughout as a living writer. I am also grateful to Dr. Anders Ryberg and the staff of the Swedish Academy's Nobel Library for their unfailing help. I have received a travel grant from *Hilda Kumlins Resestipendier*, administered by Uppsala University, which enabled me to spend some time in London, and the Department of English, Stockholm University, permitted me to spend part of an academic term doing research in London. To these and many others who have supported me during this work I wish to extend my heartfelt thanks.

Ishrat Lindblad

Stockholm University

Acknowledgment

The author wishes to thank Pamela Hansford Johnson for permission to quote from all her published works.

Chronology

In the case of the works the dates given are those of the first publication unless otherwise stated.

1912   Born in London. Father, Reginald Kenneth Johnson, and mother, Amy Clotilda, née Howson. Educated at Clapham County Secondary School, London.

1919   Sister, Beryl, born and died of marasmus five months later.

1923   Father dies.

1929   Takes six-month secretarial course at the Triangle Secretarial College, London.

1930–1934 Worked as stenographer at the London office of the Central Hanover Bank and Trust Company.

1934   Meets Victor Neuburg and joins his literary circle. Wins Sunday Referee prize for best new poem, "Chelsea Reach." *Symphony for Full Orchestra*. Meets Dylan Thomas and was briefly engaged to him.

1935   *This Bed Thy Centre*.

1936   *Blessed Above Women*. Marries Gordon Neil Stewart. Begins contributing to *John O'London's Weekly* and *Liverpool Post*.

1937   *Here Today* and *World's End*.

1938   *The Monument*.

1939–1945 War years spent at Staines.

1939   *Girdle of Venus*.

1940   *Too Dear for My Possessing* and *Tidy Death* (as Nap Lombard in collaboration with Neil Stewart).

1941   Son, Andrew Morven, born.

1942   *The Family Pattern*.

1943   *Winter Quarters* and *Murder's a Swine* (as Nap Lombard, American title *The Grinning Pig*, 1943).

1944	Frequent broadcasts for the British Broadcasting Corporation, notably as a reviewer of books until her death. Daughter, Lindsay Jean, born. *The Trojan Brothers.*
1947	Contributor to the *Sunday Chronicle*. *An Avenue of Stone* and *Thomas Wolfe* (American title *Hungry Gulliver*, 1948).
1948–1956	*Six Proust Reconstructions* broadcast: "The Duchess at Sunset," 1948; "Swann in Love," 1952; "Madame de Charlus," 1954; "Albertine Regained," 1954; "Saint-Loup," 1955; and "A Window at Montjaurin," 1956.
1948	Divorced from Gordon Neil Stewart. *A Summer to Decide. Corinth House* performed at the New Lindsey Theatre, London.
1949–1950	Regular contributor to the *Daily Telegraph* (mainly as a reviewer of books).
1949	*The Philistines.*
1950	Marries Charles Percy Snow (Lord Snow).
1951	Six plays written in collaboration with C. P. Snow: *The Supper Dance, Family Party, Spare the Rod, To Murder Mrs. Mortimer, The Pigeon with the Silver Foot,* and *Her Best Foot Forward.* Appointed Fellow Royal Society of Literature, London.
1952	Moves for a time to Clare, Suffolk. Son, Philip Charles Hansford Snow, born. *Catherine Carter.*
1953	*Ivy Compton-Burnett.*
1954	Mother dies. First trip to Canada and the United States. *Corinth House* and *An Impossible Marriage.*
1956	*The Last Resort* (American title *The Sea and the Wedding*, 1957).
1958	*Six Proust Reconstructions* (American title *Proust Recaptured: Six Radio Sketches Based on the Author's Characters*).
1959	*The Humbler Creation* and *The Unspeakable Skipton.*
1961	*The Rehearsal* in collaboration with Kitty Black. An adaptation of a play by Jean Anouilh performed in London and published. Appointed Fellow of the Center

for Advanced Studies, Wesleyan University, Middletown, Connecticut, and Honorary Fellow, Timothy Dwight College, Yale University, New Haven, Connecticut.

1962   *An Error of Judgement.*

1963   *Night and Silence, Who Is Here? An American Comedy.* Member of the Societé Européene de Culture. D. Litt., Temple University, Philadelphia.

1965   *Cork Street, Next to the Hatter's: A Novel in Bad Taste.*

1967   *On Iniquity: Some Personal Reflections Arising Out of the Moors Murder Trial. The Public Prosecutor* in collaboration with C. P. Snow. An adaptation of a play by Georgi Dzhagarov translated by Marguerite Alexieva. Performed in London. D. Litt., York University, Toronto, Canada.

1968   *The Survival of the Fittest.*

1969   *The Public Prosecutor.*

1970   *The Honours Board.* Honorary Degree, Widener College, Chester, Pennsylvania.

1972   *The Holiday Friend.*

1974   *Important to Me: Personalia.*

1975   *The Good Listener.* Created Commander of the British Empire.

1978   *The Good Husband.*

1979   Work in progress: a novel, "Adelaide Bartlett."

1980   Husband, C. P. Snow, dies.

1981   *A Bonfire.* June 19, Pamela Hansford Johnson dies.

Chapter One

Introduction

Pamela Hansford Johnson has stated that "no novelist should attempt to write his full autobiography—he has written himself and his life into his novels, no matter how much both are disguised."[1] Many people would go further and say that nobody should attempt to probe into the details of an author's life in an effort to gain insight into the works. Nevertheless, there is something to be gained by learning of those aspects of an author's life that seem to have influenced his choice of situations, characters, and motifs. Pamela Hansford Johnson, for example, often uses a comparatively trifling detail from life in a way that adds to the realistic effect of the world she creates in her fiction. She also does not hesitate to use real people in a recognizable way as the source of some of her characters. This is especially true of the semiautobiographical novel *The Survival of the Fittest*, which contains characters resembling Dame Edith Sitwell, Mikhail Sholokov, Dylan Thomas, and herself. She is also aware of another self-portrait in the character of Christine in *An Impossible Marriage* (1954).

Readers of her work who are interested in the facts that have contributed to Pamela Hansford Johnson's development as a writer will learn a great deal from her own collection of memorabilia entitled *Important to Me*, 1974 (hereafter, *Imp.*). The existence of this book makes it unnecessary to try to sketch a conventional life in this chapter. I have chosen instead to focus on only those details that have obviously been used in her novels, or which provide some insight into her concerns as a novelist.

Pamela Hansford Johnson was born in London on May 29, 1912. One of her earliest emotional experiences was a sense of guilt. In *Important to Me* she admits that "I am always guilty about something. Guilt has been my besetting misfortune, a torment to attack me at the strangest moments" (pp. 14–15). She traces her earliest experience of this emotion back to the age of seven when she lost her baby sister, Beryl. This sister was born without her having been at all prepared for the baby's arrival. Not only did she suffer the usual feelings of sibling rivalry, she was also unable to feel sorrow when the baby sister died five months later: "It was the beginning of guilt" (p. 22). Indeed the pangs of guilt are severely felt and accurately described in many of her books.

The death of her sister was not the only early tragedy Pamela Hansford Johnson had to face. Her father, a government servant who worked for the Nigerian Railway and spent a great deal of his time abroad, died suddenly while on home leave when she was only eleven years old. His death left his widow, Amy Clotilda, and his daughter in comparatively impoverished circumstances. Consequently the first twenty years of her life were spent in the shabby-genteel suburb of Clapham. The knowledge that she gained of the dreariness of suburban life and of the problems of the lower middle class has stood her in good stead as a writer. The world of her novels is often the world of London's shabbier and more depressing suburbs, and the people that she writes about know the fear of unemployment and the deadening routine of suburban life.

Unable to afford private schooling or a university education, Pamela Hansford Johnson was fortunate in attending a good state grammar school, the Clapham County Secondary School. Here she learned to appreciate literature and art. One of the art teachers, Miss Hedgeland, was responsible for instilling an enduring love of painting in her receptive pupil. Pamela Hansford Johnson often describes people in her books by comparing them to figures in the work of the great masters. She also describes scenery with a remarkable eye for visual detail and color. The characters in her books are art critics or painters as often as they are writers or people with literary talent. Her knowledge of literature (both English and

French) is the result of self-teaching. She has, however, paid Aldous Huxley the compliment (*Imp.*, p. 82) of having "opened miraculous doors" to her through his anthology with critical commentaries entitled *Texts and Pretexts* (1933).

On her first trip to Belgium with her mother and aunt at the age of fifteen, Miss Johnson found ample nourishment for her appetite for art. She has a special predilection for Flemish painting and she fell lastingly in love with Belgium itself. She uses the town of Bruges as the setting of two of her most important novels, *Too Dear for My Possessing* (1941) and *The Unspeakable Skipton* (1959). She also uses the Belgian coast as the setting of one of her more recent novels, *The Holiday Friend* (1972).

Leaving school at the age of sixteen, Miss Johnson attended secretarial school and found herself employment at the age of eighteen with the Central Hanover Bank and Trust Company in London. Throughout this time she was trying to write. She cannot, in fact, remember when she actually started to write. The first thing she can recall is a *pièce d'occasion* written at the age of six for the birthday of an aunt.[2] She also grew up in an atmosphere which must have encouraged creativity. Her maternal grandfather, Charles E. Howson, was treasurer to Sir Henry Irving for twenty-five years; her aunt toured with Sir Henry in America; and her mother joined the D'Oyly Carte Opera Company. Naturally enough Pamela Hansford Johnson's first ambition was to be an actress, but, listening to the advice of her experienced family, she abandoned the thought and concentrated her talents on writing instead. She also began to acquire literary contacts and her real opening came through one of them. This was Victor Neuburg, an eccentric journalist who kept open house for poets and had obtained the editorship of a column in the *Sunday Referee* entitled "The Poet's Corner." He published Pamela Hansford Johnson's poems, and one of them, "Chelsea Reach," won the *Sunday Referee*'s annual prize, which was the subsidization of a book of poems. This book, *Symphony for Full Orchestra*, marked her literary debut.

Victor Neuburg was not only responsible for providing her with this professional opening, he was also responsible for her first

meeting with Dylan Thomas. On a visit to London, Dylan Thomas's
closest friend, Daniel Jones, attended one of Neuburg's gatherings
and upon his return to Wales regaled Dylan Thomas with a somewhat pejorative account of it.[3] Ready to seize any opportunity that
offered itself, Dylan Thomas immediately submitted a poem to "The
Poet's Corner" which both won an annual prize and solicited
Pamela Hansford Johnson's admiration in the form of a letter. A
regular correspondence arose between the two even before they met
in London, and soon after their first meeting a romance blossomed.
It was to be shortlived, however, and after a brief engagement the
two parted as friends. Dylan Thomas wrote a great many letters to
Pamela Hansford Johnson during their courtship and all of these
have been preserved and deposited at the Lockwood Memorial
Library in Buffalo, New York. Unfortunately, none of her replies
to Dylan Thomas has been preserved, but there is a diary that she
kept during this time.[4] The two seem to have discussed poetry a
great deal together and there must have been a certain amount of
mutual influence. The title of her first novel, *This Bed Thy Centre*
(1935), was suggested by Dylan Thomas. One of her early short
stories was entitled "Altarwise by Owl-light" and quoted the relevant lines from Dylan Thomas's poem as an epigraph. The narrative technique of some of her early novels is also reminiscent of
Dylan Thomas's although in this case both of them were probably
exploiting trends current at that time. *Winter Quarters* (1944), for
example, uses parallel plots in a way that recalls *Under Milkwood*,
but the latter was not published before 1954.

The group of young writers among whom Pamela Hansford
Johnson was moving during the 1930s were at the center of the
cultural and intellectual life of that time. The poets of the 1930s
(notably W. H. Auden, Stephen Spender, and Hugh MacDiarmid)
provide a key to the period as a whole—the increased suspicion of
fascism and the widespread response to the Spanish Civil War.
There is no doubt that Pamela Hansford Johnson shared the political commitment of this generation. She was a member of the Chelsea Labour party and the Left Book Club, and edited a weekly
called the *Chelsea Democrat* from the party headquarters in the

World's End (*Imp.*, p. 127). She also took part in demonstrations supporting the loyalists in Spain.

The mood of the 1930s is captured in many of her novels. Her protagonists espouse socialistic ideals; many of her young men leave Britain in order to go to fight in Spain for the Republican cause, and the shadow of the two world wars is cast over almost every book that she sets in that period. Pamela Hansford Johnson clearly feels that the lives of individuals are inextricably bound up with the major historical events of their time, and it is equally clear that the events of the 1930s were crucial to her work.

In 1936, Pamela Hansford Johnson married an Australian-born journalist and historian named Gordon Neil Stewart. Her mother, with whom she had developed an unusually close relationship, moved into her daughter's new home. After the marriage Pamela Hansford Johnson continued to write regularly, publishing a new book each year for the next five or six years. She also wrote two books with her husband under the pseudonym Nap Lombard. Both of these are murder stories that fall outside the pattern established by the serious novels she publishes in her own name. During this time she also began to contribute regularly to magazines and newspapers and to broadcast for the British Broadcasting Corporation.

Not long after her marriage, the Second World War broke out and her husband was sent to serve in India. He scarcely saw their two children, a son, Andrew Morven, born in 1941, and a daughter, Lindsay Jean, born in 1944. Upon receiving his discharge in 1946 he returned home to his family, but tensions arose among him, his wife, and his mother-in-law. Eventually he and his wife agreed to divorce.

In 1950 Pamela Hansford Johnson married the novelist Charles Percy Snow (Lord Snow), an old friend of her family's for whose work she had previously expressed admiration in articles and reviews.[5] The two of them wrote several short plays together, but, according to her own description, these were written in a frivolous mood during their honeymoon and are not to be taken seriously.

After their marriage the couple moved for a time to Clare, Suffolk, where their son, Philip Charles, was born. In Cambridgeshire she came into contact with the academic world to which her husband belonged and a recent novel, *The Good Listener* (1975), reveals her insight into the university life of Cambridge.

The fact that C. P. Snow is a highly successful writer has not, according to Pamela Hansford Johnson herself, created problems between them but served rather as a bond.[6] Even so, she has written an interesting story entitled "My Books Are My Children" (1955), in which she imaginatively explores the tensions that can arise when a successful female author marries an author who has become a cult.

At the time of her second marriage Pamela Hansford Johnson asked her husband whether or not her mother should continue to live with them. His decision that she should is one that Miss Johnson describes as "splendidly unselfish, but I am not sure that it turned out to be wise" (*Imp.*, p. 115). She had already experienced the tensions that arose in her first marriage on account of the hostility her mother felt toward her daughter's husband (*Imp.*, pp. 80–81, 121). In several novels the case of a single parent—mother, father, or stepmother—who has come to mean a great deal to the child and with whom the child continues to share a home recurs. The parent becomes possessive and demanding and the child is unable to liberate himself from a situation which inevitably affects his ability to form other successful relationships.

Another recurrent motif which seems related to Pamela Hansford Johnson's own experience is that of a parent (or a loved one) being left to die alone. In *Important to Me*, Johnson has given an extremely candid account of her own feelings when her mother died alone in Cambridge while she was herself in London for professional reasons. The fact that people are often left to die alone and the ones who have been closest to them are overcome with severe feelings of guilt is an indication of the significance of this experience to her work as a writer.

After her mother's death in 1952, Lord and Lady Snow spent a great deal of time traveling together—to the Soviet Union, where they met Mikhail Sholokov; to Canada and the United States, where they have received academic honors and enjoy great esteem.

Miss Johnson has made comic use of some of her experience as a writer in residence at an American university in one of her rare satirical novels, *Night and Silence, Who Is Here?*

From the 1950s onward, in fact, Pamela Hansford Johnson's reputation as a distinguished novelist has been taken for granted even though it is difficult to pinpoint the moment when such general recognition was awarded. A reviewer writing about her work in 1959 put it very well when he suggested that she belonged "to that group of writers—they are perhaps most to be envied—whose fame has climbed slowly on the wings of each new achievement. In the past ten years she has become well known to the reading public as a novelist of great craftsmanship and distinction and to the readers of the weeklies as one of the best contemporary reviewers of novels in the language."[7] This is a judgment that can very well be applied today.

Pamela Hansford Johnson has continued to produce impressive novels that testify to her seriousness of purpose without making a great stir by the publication of a universally acclaimed masterpiece. She has not followed the current trend toward innovative fiction that is so prevalent in America and has consequently been regarded as a "traditional" English novelist.

A reviewer in *Newsweek* expresses this attitude in a review of *Survival of the Fittest*: "Only in England do serious and sophisticated writers still compose long, densely populated, intransigently realistic novels that chronicle the life cycle of a generation against a historical background still fresh in the memory without conceding an inch of bloody territory to any literary fashion past or passing or to come."[8] Although the reviewer is clearly expressing disapprobation, Pamela Hansford Johnson has consciously chosen to follow "the great tradition" of the English novel. In fact she deplores the modernist tendency to experiment with form at the cost of content.[9] In an article entitled "The Sick-room Hush over the English Novel" (1949), she defends her concept of what is worthwhile in the British tradition: "The great novels of the world have been stories about human beings, deeply and fully realised, living the major experiences of their lives in the surroundings of their time. . . .

The English tradition in the novel, fathered by Chaucer, has been a peculiarly rich and robust one, an earthy tradition, instinct with the odour of man, growing up out of the unique temperament of a people. It has, in every sense, been a popular art."[10] It is this tradition that she herself strives to emulate in her own art.

Chapter Two

The Novels of Suburbia

The world that Pamela Hansford Johnson created in her first novel, *This Bed Thy Centre*, was the world that she knew best. In her own words: "I had thought of the novel simply as an attempt to tell the truth about a group of people in a London suburb, whose lives were arbitrarily linked."[1] The "suburb" has today become part of greater London—the area around Clapham Common, and Battersea —but it is the quality of life as lived by people in the shabbier parts of southern London that is a major subject in both her first and her third novels. *This Bed Thy Centre* (1935) and *Here Today* (1937) are more closely related to each other than to the other novels. In fact, as Isabel Quigly has already pointed out, "in *Here Today* Pamela Hansford Johnson frankly repeated herself for what seems to have been the only time."[2] Both these novels create the ambience of a prewar London suburb with a great deal of realism. To a large extent the books give the impression of recording the daily flow of these ordinary people's existence—"a story of the small life," as the author herself terms it in the epigraph on the title page of *Here Today*. The title itself suggests the same idea and is quoted as part of the epigraph and again in the novel by one of the minor characters: "'Ere to-day and gone to-morrow and the world not a penny the worse."[3]

This Bed Thy Centre was written, like most of Johnson's novels, within a few months. Only a month after its completion it had been accepted for publication by Chapman and Hall, and its appearance created a remarkable stir. Looking back, in her preface to the second edition, Johnson recalls how the reception it was given shocked and terrified her (p. 6). People were startled by her frank treatment of the taboo-ridden subject of sex. Writing in *John O'London's Weekly*, Richard Church feels it is set "in a world of drunken and lewd suburbia, filling the reader with nausea and speculation as to when the Hour of Sanitation will come to flow over and obliterate the squalor of scenes in pubs and back streets and the minds of pimply, adolescent girls."[4] Other critics hailed the appearance of a considerable talent. Cyril Connolly praises the book for the author's admirable grasp of the psychology of its characters, "their dialogue and circumstances of living,"[5] and J. S. Southron describes it as an unusually successful attempt "to render articulate the dumb longings and inchoate meanderings of thought that attend ordinary adolescence."[6] As Pamela Hansford Johnson suggests, the book "by today's standards would be considered a signal succcess, the nearest thing to it that I can think of is *Lucky Jim* in the very early fifties." (*Imp.*, p. 118).

The title is taken from a poem by John Donne, part of which is quoted on the title page. It was suggested by Dylan Thomas and, as the author herself has since realized, her original title, "Nursery Rhyme," would probably have been more appropriate (*Bed*, p. 6). In this book the author is essentially concerned with describing the break from the nursery world that adolescence involves and in order to emphasize this theme she has woven references to several well-known nursery rhymes and fairy tales into the fabric of the novel. In his review, J. S. Southron complains that the wording of some of the chapter headings "is pretentious or blatantly sensational."[7] Perhaps this would have been less noticeable if the original title had been retained. The headings could then have been related to the theme of change in the nursery. Several chapter headings like "Heigh-Ho, Says Roly," "O Saisons, O Chateaux," and "The Silver Nutmeg" allude to nursery rhymes. On several occasions the lines of such rhymes run through the heroine's head in a way that effectively indicates her response to the things around her. For example, at the beginning of the book Elsie realizes: "There was so much to learn, so much to be forgotten, such a lot of Bluebeard cupboards to be opened. A rhyme ran in her head. One, two, buckle my shoe. Three, four, open the door" (p. 54). Later, when she meets her fiancé's aunt for the first time, she is associated with Little Red Riding Hood. Aunt Rose kisses Elsie, "who shied visibly. Oh, what great teeth you have, grandmamma" (p. 265). These lines show how the author is trying to explore the inner sensibility of an adolescent on the threshold of womanhood.

The main characters in *This Bed Thy Centre* are Elsie Cotton, the sixteen-year-old daughter of Mrs. Cotton, a widow of small means, and Roly, the town councilor's son, who meets and falls in love with her. Elsie is strongly attracted to Roly but totally unprepared for the awakening of her sexual desires. She conforms rigidly to the strict morality that her mother has taught her and refuses to yield to Roly's importuning until after they are married. Roly is thus driven to infidelity first by giving in to the desire of the local prostitute, Mrs. Maginnis, and later by sleeping with Gwen, the girl from the local library. Elsie learns of his interest in Gwen, quarrels with him, and goes away on holiday with her mother. While she is away Roly's father dies. Elsie's sympathy for his loss brings about their reconciliation; they agree to become engaged and are duly married. Instead of the "happily ever after" ending of the fairy tale, however, the last few pages of the novel record the frightened thoughts of the young bride as she waits for her husband on her wedding night.

Two other love stories are interwoven with the main narrative. The first tells of the unhappiness of Mrs. Maginnis, who has wasted her life on worthless men. She clings in desperation to her latest lover, George, but he leaves her after having exploited her. Terrified of loneliness and overcome with fear when she discovers a lump in her breast, Mrs. Maginnis commits suicide after a long ritual preparation for death. Her lover, learning of her suicide, spares her a few desultory thoughts but remains unmoved by the tragedy he has caused. As a character type Mrs. Maginnis is an extremely important creation. Unconventional and flamboyant, the woman of easy virtue who has a heart of gold, she is the prototype of Helena in the "Helena" trilogy, one of the best known of all Pamela Hansford Johnson's creations (*Bed*, p. 7).

Another woman who is caught in a similarly unhappy relationship is Elsie Cotton's art-mistress, Leda Chevasse. She has been deserted by the ne'er-do-well young poet John, with whom she is in love. At first she tries to find consolation by responding with abnormal intensity to Elsie's schoolgirl passion for her, but as soon as John reappears she falls under his spell once more. She becomes pregnant, John is forced to acknowledge his responsibility for the child, and the two of them are trapped in a relationship that is unlikely to bring either of them any happiness.

Yet another unhappy family whose life is exposed is that of Mrs. Godshill, the local bigot. While preaching hell-fire and damnation to her community, she fails to see the misery she is inflicting upon her own children, Arthur and Ada Mary. Arthur shows every sign of being driven to drink like his father before him, and Ada Mary, after a vain effort to confide in Mrs. Maginnis, commits suicide by drowning herself in the local pond.

The peripheral characters—Mr. Parsons, the fruit-stall owner; Ma Ditch, the pussy butcher (cat's meat man); Masie, the pub owner; and Mr. Wilkinson, the inveterate gambler who marries Masie—circle around the central characters, commenting upon their lives and function, to some extent, in the manner of the chorus in a Greek play. They suggest the stable element in the neighborhood. Their lives go on regardless of the tragedies of the small people.

These same small people are also the subject of *Here Today*—although their individual stories are different, their world is very similar. The suburb in this book is called Wadley. The different strands of the story are divided among Miss Waghorn, the milliner; Mr. Doppy, the florist; and the two families at the two rival public houses, the Pereiras at the Childe Roland and the Simms at the less successful the Bagpipes.

Miss Waghorn's is a sordid and sad tale. She is living in Wadley under an assumed name after having been caught and convicted elsewhere for shoplifting. With painstaking effort she succeeds in establishing a modest business as a milliner until the florist, Mr. Doppy, discovers her secret and begins to black mail her.

Mr. Doppy is an evil man who enjoys victimizing people. Not only does he blackmail Miss Waghorn, but he also uses his position as Miss Tuke's employer to force her to accept his attentions and ultimately to marry him. He also tries to blackmail Bert Pereira.

Bert Pereira, the owner of the Childe Roland, betrays his wife by entering into a relationship with Miss Waghorn. Once caught in its complications, he finds it increasingly difficult to free himself. His son, Phil, realizes his father is deceiving his mother, a fact which creates a great deal of tension between the two of them. In the end Miss Waghorn leaves Wadley and Bert Pereira returns thankfully to his wife, Madge.

Young love is represented by the relationship between Phil and the daughter of the rival pub owner, Connie Simms. A well-to-do young undergraduate, Ernest Damian, arouses Phil's jealousy and threatens to come between them for a while, but by the end of the book the two of them know they love each other and plan to marry.

Narrative Technique

Although *This Bed Thy Centre* gives prominence to the story of Elsie, and *Here Today* divides attention equally among the lives of Miss Waghorn, Mr. Doppy, the Pereiras, and the Simms, both novels employ the method of parallel plots associated with Aldous Huxley's *Point Counterpoint*, or Dylan Thomas's much later play *Under Milkwood*. The local public house in each book, the Admiral Drake in the first and the Childe Roland in the second, function as gathering points for the people in the suburb. From this central nucleus the lives of the major characters spread out in a widening circle.

In her narrative technique Pamela Hansford Johnson is clearly influenced by the experimentation that went on in the arts during the 1920s and brought into being the modern psychological novel. As Leon Edel has pointed out in his study of this genre, at about the same time in history Marcel Proust, James Joyce, and Dorothy

Richardson wrote books that were each of them an expression of the
need "to record the 'inwardness' of experience."[8] The first volumes
of *Remembrance of Things Past* appeared in 1913, Joyce published
The Portrait of the Artist as a Young Man in 1914, and Dorothy
Richardson published the first volume of *Pilgrimage* in 1915. These
pioneers introduced the techniques of stream of consciousness and
interior monologue. Virginia Woolf continued the tradition and in
1928 Huxley developed the contrapuntal method in *Point Counterpoint*.

In addition to these important extensions of the range of the
novel there were many important new techniques being developed
in cinematic art that were to have an influence upon narrative
methods. David W. Griffith, the American film producer, made
Birth of a Nation in 1915 and *Intolerance* in 1916. In these two
films he developed the technique of cross-cutting known as "mon-
tage"—the use of alternate images in juxtaposition to enhance the
meaning of each. Later, in 1924, the Russian film director S. M.
Eisenstein developed Griffith's techniques even more fully in his
classic film *Battleship Potemkin*.

This outburst of creative experiment just before and during the
1920s meant that, by the time Pamela Hansford Johnson began to
write, the techniques of stream of consciousness and parallel plots
had obtained general currency.

In *This Bed Thy Centre* and *Here Today*, Pamela Hansford
Johnson's narrative focuses for a short period on a scene in the life
of one of her characters before switching to another. The juxtaposition of the two scenes enhances the meaning of each, creating a
unity that has a more complex significance than either of the two
scenes could have had in isolation. Thus, for example, there is a
brief scene in *This Bed Thy Centre* where Roly is full of appre-
hension after receiving a note from Gwen asking him to meet her
because she has something important to tell him. Without actually
expressing what it is he fears, the scene ends with his thoughts: "No,
it couldn't be" (p. 219). The next scene opens on Leda and her
lover together, and John asks her, "A child, my darling?" It proves
that Leda is pregnant. Her unwanted pregnancy is thus immedi-

ately linked to Roly's fears, and John's distaste for the role of father is a reflection on Roly as well.

Another characteristic feature of her technique is the use of interior monologues and stream of consciousness. In the *New Republic* a reviewer writes slightingly of her use of this method, describing her characters as "wading many a sluggish stream of consciousness."[9] In fact, the stream does not flow sluggishly at all. Elsie's fear of sex is built up into a kind of crescendo by the constant use of the phrases "Perfect love casteth out fear" and "Oh God, I don't want to get married" in the middle of her fervent efforts to think about something else. Mrs. Maginnis's fear of cancer is also best expressed by rendering the flow of her thoughts.

In *Here Today*, Miss Waghorn's fear of her guilty secret being discovered, Mr. Doppy's malevolent delight in persecuting his victims, Bert Pereira's despair at the thought of his wife's finding out about his infidelity, and Phil's emotions as he stands waiting to meet Connie are all conveyed directly to the reader by using a technique that gives the impression of their innermost thoughts being recorded.

Related to this technique is the frequent use of *erlebte rede*, or indirect direct speech. For example, Mrs. Maginnis returns to her lonely room after an attempt at forced gaiety in the pub. She bumps into a gramophone: "As the instrument crashed down, the needle gave a last scream up the record. I hope no one heard. They'll be coming to ask questions, and I can't talk to them. She touched herself with fearful fingers" (p. 98). Here the word "scream" indicates how it sounded to Mrs. Maginnis, and "I hope no one heard. They'll be coming to ask questions" is a direct transcription of her thoughts without the use of quotation marks, and it imperceptibly gives way to the third-person narration of "She touched herself with fearful fingers." Thus the description of a simple episode like a gramophone falling to the floor assumes the same proportions for the reader as it has for the person involved. The use of lines from songs and poems as refrains that stick in the minds of her characters and suddenly interrupt their thoughts, and the frequent recounting of dreams and nightmares are other ways of rendering events of internal rather than external importance.

In both these early novels the prose is frequently poetic. Thus Mr. Doppy in his flower shop is described: "He touched his great stone jar full of delphiniums, evil blue, wedding blue, sleeping purple. Nice" (p. 14). There are several lyrical descriptions of the Common where Roly and Elsie take their walks and, in both novels, poetic images abound. In *Here Today*, for example, a passage of description uses the image "wands of light lengthen with the green evening" (p. 13). This use of language reveals Miss Hansford Johnson's early interest in poetry and her use, in prose, of many of the stylistic techniques of the poet.

A detail of technique which becomes increasingly apparent through its frequent use in other novels is the description of the immediate surroundings in terms of the mood of the person who is involved. Thus when Elsie is out walking with Roly she looks up at "the bewildering trees" (*Bed*, p. 127) and later she sees "the night as if it were the drowning waters into which the girl had stepped" (*Bed*, p. 243).

The technique of these early novels has been analyzed in some detail because it is used again in several novels, and in subsequent chapters examples from the other novels can be added to supplement the picture already gained from this discussion.

Situations and Themes

The early novels are seminal in that they also contain recurrent situations and themes. A detail that becomes more and more noticeable in her later work is the way in which her characters frequently look in a mirror to take stock of the image with which they are presented. Thus in an important scene Elsie, left alone in her home on a Saturday afternoon, undresses and swathes her body in a counterpane as an expression of her awakened sensuality (p. 102). Roly examines his face in the mirror after having made love to Mrs. Maginnis, and Elsie looks at herself when she is miserable with jealousy of Gwen, and again on her wedding day to see if it reflects any of the changes within her. The use of a mirror recurs so frequently in her novels as to suggest it has a special significance for the author as a symbol. It reflects human beings in the same way that art itself does.

Two subjects which have a very minor place in the first novel yet come to be extremely important in later novels are those of art and those of the relationship between mother and child. John is an aspiring poet and Leda is an art-mistress. In one of the art lessons she teaches Elsie that art offers creative freedom: "You can paint leaves blue, if you like. There's no limitation at all, and anything's permissible in design" (p. 31). This statement is important enough to be used as the title of the chapter in which it is contained. However, it does not apply to anything that Elsie does later in the novel and is a rather revealing example of a phrase that could have had structural significance but remains an isolated observation. In *Here Today* the subject of art does not enter the novel, but in subsequent novels the major characters frequently have literary and artistic ambitions and move in bohemian artistic circles.

The relationship between Elsie and her mother is a prototype of many similar relationships between parent and child in the later novels. Mrs. Cotton is a widow and it is easy for her to be too possessive about her daughter. She makes Elsie feel guilty for leaving her mother alone when she marries. The problem of jealousy and conflict between Roly and his mother-in-law-to-be is raised but not fully developed. This kind of situation is one that Johnson frequently describes and it is therefore worth noting it even when it plays a relatively minor part.

In both *This Bed Thy Centre* and *Here Today* there is a strong undercurrent of violence, perversity, and tragedy beneath the surface of suburban life. In *This Bed Thy Centre* some of this is suggested through the suicides of Ada Mary and Mrs. Maginnis. Mrs. Maginnis's suppressed suffering is momentarily revealed when Roly gives her a bunch of flowers. She is so overcome by the painful nature of the memories they arouse that she grinds one of the flowers that has fallen "into the linoleum with her foot, as if she were setting her heel in the face of a dead enemy" (p. 240).

In the same way in *Here Today* there is violence in Wadley. Mrs. Waghorn's first husband dies in tragic circumstances after his wife has been tried for shoplifting. Mr. Doppy dies a violent death by falling on the spikes of one of his conical funeral vases when he trips on the matting in his shop in order to avoid a blow from Bert Pereira's son. Connie Simms's younger brother, Rob, is a deformed boy who reacts with violence to the things he cannot understand. He hangs his teddy-bear in a cupboard, shocking his sister by this action (p. 205), and later he attacks Phil, mistaking him for Mr. Doppy, whom he dislikes instinctively. Mr. Doppy is interested in Connie and tries to gain her favor by giving her handicapped brother flowers (pp. 210–11). However, Rob realizes they are wilted and would have to be thrown away.

Perversity is reflected in the relationship between Elsie and her art teacher. The love that the pupil feels makes her suffer sharp pangs of jealousy when John comes back to monopolize Leda. Leda is also drawn to Elsie and a climax in their relationship is reached in a scene where Leda kisses Elsie with violent passion after having detained her for some trivial offense in the classroom.

Much of this violence and perversity can be linked to a criticism of the stifling mentality reflected in the suburb as a whole. Roly, in *This Bed Thy Centre*, voices some of this criticism when he argues with Elsie on the subject of premarital sex: "It's the whole social system that's at fault. . . . When a man loves a woman he ought to be able to sleep with her right away, and then there would be no repressions or inhibitions or anything" (p. 284). He is also the one to object most strongly to Elsie's dependence upon her mother and opposes any suggestion that his mother-in-law should come to live with them after their marriage. Even though Roly uses these arguments to help him to accomplish his own ends, the emphasis placed on Elsie's fear of her wedding night and her own involuntary thought, "If only I could have loved him when I wanted to" (p. 316), suggests that the author wishes to draw attention to the taboo-ridden world in which Elsie has been brought up.

An aspect of suburban life which is lightly touched upon in these two novels but which becomes an increasingly important subject in later novels is an awareness of class and of social problems. Elsie's mother is extremely conscious of Roly's being the town councilor's son who can help her daughter to climb a step up the social ladder. When she is invited to tea by his aunt, she feels ill at ease and acutely aware of her inferior social status.

In *Here Today* three charwomen sit in the pub and discuss the way society is organized. The most radical of them, Mrs. Babcock, is the one who makes the statement that lends its title to the novel. She is also the one to object to the existing scheme of things: " 'Them fine bitches,' said Mrs. Babcock venemously, 'ought to 'ave to live in one room with a kid, go out all day to scrub till their nice white 'ands break out in sores and then spend 'arf the night fighting the bugs or trying to sleep with the smell of sulphur-candles in the blankets. That would do 'em good.' 'Oh, I wouldn't go so far as that,' said Mrs. Hooper, who was of gentler mind. 'After all, they ain't brought up to scrub and they do give employment' " (p. 27). These characters suggest that society needs reform but they do not affect the purpose of the novel, which is simply to describe life in Wadley as it is without making any overt judgments on its condition.

The last chapter in *This Bed Thy Centre* describes changes in the neighborhood and tries to relate these to the changes that have taken place in the individual lives described. However, the chapter is not integrated with the rest of the novel. It shows how Pamela Hansford Johnson wishes to relate the lives of individual people to events in a larger social framework, but it also shows her failure to fuse the private and the public world into an artistic whole.

Both *This Bed Thy Centre* and *Here Today* are examples of some of Johnson's lasting concerns as a novelist. The type of suburb she has created in these two novels becomes a familiar setting to the reader who delves deeper into her work. The emphasis on unhappiness may create a depressing picture, but it is undoubtedly part of the world she has chosen to describe. In these early novels she fashions a narrative technique that she uses in several novels before moving on to a more chronological method of narration. The next group of novels to be discussed reveals many of the characteristics already analyzed but extends her range considerably. It is to these more assured and accomplished novels that attention is directed in the next chapter.

Chapter Three

Radicals and Bohemians in the 1930s

In the two novels discussed in the previous chapter, Pamela Hansford Johnson created a picture of the type of suburb in which she spent her childhood. In *World's End* (1937), *The Monument* (1938), and *The Survival of the Fittest* (1968), she makes use of the environment in which she came of age. She leaves Clapham and enters Chelsea and Bloomsbury. The world she wishes to create is now the world of young left-wing intellectuals in the 1930s in England, which were not solely a time of depression and impending catastrophe. Johnson points this out in her discussion of politics and war in *Important to Me*: "To the young the years leading up to the war and the earlier years of the war itself, may have been days of acute anxiety and activity, but they were often fun. Great fun. The problems for the Left were simple: you didn't like Hitler, nor Mussolini, nor Franco" (p. 127). Thus the group of friends who have lived through this period together in *The Survival of the Fittest* looks back on it with nostalgic pleasure as "the wild life." Although the period in all three books to be discussed in this chapter is the same, *World's End* is different from both *The Monument* and *The Survival of the Fittest* in that Arnold Brand, the protagonist, experiences more of the difficulties of the 1930s, the unemployment and insecurity, than the fun.

The very first book in which Pamela Hansford Johnson introduces the life of bohemians in London is actually her second novel,

Blessed Above Women. This book is discussed elsewhere on account of the main theme being quite different from that of the novels to be analyzed here. However, it is worth pointing out that in *Blessed Above Women* one of the main characters, Joah Sullivan, hopes to be a novelist and comes to live in London. He and his bohemian friends spend their time in pubs and a studio near Bloomsbury. One of them is a remarkably talented painter, and the other a progressive young woman who defies the conventional moral code. The life they lead is similar to the life of the group of friends who are the main characters in *The Survival of the Fittest,* but whereas it plays a small part in the earlier novel, it becomes a major one in the later novel.

World's End is set in the seedy, semiartistic district of World's End, Chelsea, which gives the novel its name. Although the district exists in fact, its name has definite metaphorical implications. As the reveiwer in the *Times Literary Supplement* was quick to note, the people in the story "live in World's End in more senses than one"; they are "surrounded by a terrifying sense that all ordered life is hovering uncertainly on the brink of disaster."[1] This awareness of events in the world at large was probably one of the reasons why many critics felt that *World's End* was a greater novel than any of Johnson's previous ones. E. H. Walton, for example, spoke of her having "suddenly acquired new depth and maturity."[2] In *World's End* she succeeds in telling a moving, personal story at the same time as she shows how the major events of the time affect the lives of ordinary people.

The story of Arnold Brand's life is one of struggle against the evils of unemployment during the slump in the 1930s. A well-educated young man with literary ambitions, he is unable to find a job. His wife, Doris, has a miserable job as a salesgirl in a small shop, and the couple is forced to make do on her pitiful wages. In spite of their difficulties, their marriage has remained fresh over a period of nine years. However, a crisis is impending, and it comes in the shape of a momentary infatuation. Brand is attracted to a young dancer, Rosemary, partly because she enables Brand to regain some of his self-respect. His situation becomes increasingly impossible and finally he decides to confide in his wife. This results in the loss of her love just when he needs it most. She learns to love him again, but too late. Doris is expecting a child, and it is only on her way to the delivery room that she feels a renewal of her love for Arnold. Their happiness is extremely shortlived, however, for she dies in labor. Overcome with grief, Brand leaves World's End in order to join the International Brigade and fight in Spain.

Although Johnson continues to use the technique of parallel plots in this novel, the focus is clearly on Arnold Brand and his wife, and all the other characters whose lives are touched upon and form part of their social network. Sipe, Brand's closest friend, is a gifted pianist who has been driven to drink by the desertion of his beautiful and well-to-do wife, Irene. Rosemary, a chorus girl, lives a squalid life with a drunken mother and a talented younger sister. She falls genuinely in love with Brand, but there is no future for her in this relationship. Ma Hogben is Brand's good-natured Cockney landlady, and she comforts him and Doris when they need it. Her life is also touched by tragedy. Unable to keep his job, her husband commits suicide, but Ma Hogben accepts his death with simple good faith.

All these people are aware of world events in the 1930s. Brand's earliest memory is of the way Old Black the baker was mobbed by the boys in his school when word was spread that he was a German spy. Ma Hogben speaks with horror of the persecution of the Jews in Germany and Sipe tells of a meeting in the Albert Hall where anti-Semitic feeling was rife. MacDonald, who also lodges in Ma Hogben's house, is a member of the Communist party and helps to make Brand aware of the social injustices that prevail. It is largely through his influence that Brand decides to fight for Spain. One of the chapters in the book is devoted to a diarylike recording of the major events in the period (Chapter 17). In this way a sense of history being made is effectively conveyed, and world events overshadow the lives of the people in World's End.

Brand's final decision to join hands with Spain is foreshadowed by several incidents earlier in the book which show his heroic nature. He jumps into the river to try to save Mr. Hogben from drowning. Then he gets rid of Irene's aggressive lover when he threatens Sipe. On the third occasion his behavior is contrasted with MacDonald's. On his way home from a walk with Doris, they see a child balanced on a window-ledge in the building opposite their own. She is fast asleep. Brand immediately tries to climb up the facade in an effort to save her before she falls. MacDonald is more rational, however, and fetches a fire ladder which enables him to rescue the girl. Brand feels that he "swashbuckles" while Mac-Donald "acts" and is thus critical of his own type of heroism. It is difficult to decide whether the incident is intended to reveal the futility of Brand's heroism or to suggest that his kind of spontaneous bravery is the only way in which ordinary people can react in times of crisis. There is no guide to the way in which the author wishes the reader to interpret the scene.

The same period in history is used as the background of *The Monument*, but in this book Pamela Hansford Johnson distributes the interest more evenly among the lives of four people. Like *World's End*, the monument that gives the book its title has an actual geographical location and is also a metaphor. At the beginning, middle, and end of the book, the author uses the device of an omniscient narrator. He stands at the top of the tower in London, and makes a random choice among the people below to see whose story he will tell. The "four representative fish" he catches in his net are Mary Captor, a successful novelist; Annie Sellars, a poor working-class woman with a passion for left-wing politics; Rafael Barradane, the son of a wealthy Jewish businessman; and Albert Whye, an impoverished clerk. The two women and two men are obviously meant to contrast with each other, and the book is carefully structured to alternate among the four characters. It is divided into two parts of twelve chapters each. The first part is dominated by the story of Mary and Rafael and the second by the story of Albert Whye. The book begins with a glimpse of all four of them gathered together at the top of the monument. Then their lives separate. The next four chapters sketch in the background of each in retrospect. After this the story of their lives is unfolded until the middle of the book, when they are arbitrarily gathered together for a moment, then scattered again until the final assembly at the end. The narrator deliberately refuses to give the story a neat ending. In this book Pamela Hansford Johnson is clearly experimenting with the narrator's voice, but the effect is a little too contrived to be completely successful.

Mary Captor is the first character in Johnson's fiction who seems to be based on autobiographical material. A highly imaginative child, she grows up living with her mother and aunt. At school she develops a love of literature and afterwards takes a secretarial post. At the age of eighteen she completes her first novel, which enjoys a considerable *succès d'estime*. She is offered a job with the Hircus Press and becomes friends with the director, Stanley Bunker, who has established himself as a poet, and with an artist named Janaceth.

In *The Monument* the author tries to create a full picture of the joys and frustrations of artistic creation through Mary. She describes Mary's excitement and anxiety when the book she has been working on is due to be published and her misery when some of the reviews are critical and it is considered sordid and ugly. Mary is also politically active. A member of the local Labour party, she regularly takes part in their meetings and demonstrations. When she meets Rafael she is determined to like him on principle because he is a Jew and she is fighting anti-Semitism, but as a Socialist she is also bound to disapprove of his wealth. Her attitude toward him is ambivalent until she suddenly realizes that she has fallen in love with him.

Rafael Barradane is unusual in Pamela Hansford Johnson's early fiction because of his wealth and class. He lives with his widowed father, Marcus, in great material comfort and is interested in art and music. He is attracted to Mary but unsure of the depth of his feelings, and while he hesitates Mary falls in love with an attractive young man, Carel Constant, to whom she becomes engaged. Rafael's jealous reaction makes him realize he is in love with Mary. He tells her so just before leaving for Paris. Mary is wise enough to realize that she really loves Rafael. She breaks off her engagement and goes to find Rafael in Paris, where they are married. Carel dies in a plane crash and Mary makes a romantic image of the man she once loved which estranges her from Rafael for awhile. The crises in their marriage are all comparatively trivial but reveal both Mary's character and Rafael's ability to understand her.

To a large extent Mary is presented through her husband's eyes. He watches and analyzes her character and helps her through her personal crises as an author and a politician. Together the two of them succeed in creating a marriage that is deeply satisfying to them both.

Annie Sellars's life is linked with Mary's through her interest in politics. Both of them attend the meetings of the Labour party and once Mary learns of her circumstances she helps Mrs. Sellars to find employment and security as housekeeper to one of the party leaders. Annie fell in love with her husband during the First World War. She grew up with a widowed mother who moved in with her daughter and her son-in-law when they married. The arrangement caused some friction but Mrs. Selkirk died within a few years and Bob and Annie also succeed in making an unusually successful marriage. Bob Sellars has to fight against the problem of unemployment in the same way that Brand has to in *World's End*. He gets a job as a fire watchman but is badly burned during a fire in which he acts with great heroism, and is disabled for the rest of his life. Annie has to provide for her husband and two children in the same way that Doris has to provide for Arnold Brand.

Albert Whye's life never comes into direct contact with the lives of the other three characters. His is the most bleak and miserable life of them all. Burdened with an ailing and cantankerous father, Jim, and a delinquent younger brother, Teddy, he loses the girl he wishes to marry because he is never free to go out with her and cannot offer her a home of her own. Left alone, he centers all his love on his younger brother, who has been in trouble with the police once and still keeps bad company. Albert's father has always hated his youngest son and gradually Albert finds out why. The father suspects that Teddy is not really his own son because his wife was unfaithful to him shortly before she began to expect him. Jim is always threatening to beat Teddy and in the end when he finds that Teddy has stolen money from his cashbox he decides to give him up to the police. Finding that he cannot dissuade his father, Albert becomes desperate and murders him. Sitting comfortably in their home in Hampstead, Mary reads of the parricide in a news-, paper that Rafael has brought in, and the two of them discuss the news item as if it has no relation to their own lives.[3]

Although the central characters in *The Monument* are new ones, Arnold Brand makes two appearances in the book. He attends the meetings of the Labour party and acts with a presence of mind that fits well with his heroic impulses as revealed in *World's End*. On one occasion he helps Mrs. Sellars and runs one of the trouble-makers out of the hall (p. 178). On another he helps Rafael, who has become involved in a fight with some anti-Semitic dissidents at the meeting. Brand's past history is rapidly sketched in: "When his young wife died in childbirth, Brand had gone desperately to Spain with no impulse in his head but to find a cause into which he had thrown his whole physical strength. He had returned with his whole mind given to the Spanish people for whose freedom he had fought" (p. 181). Interestingly enough, the importance of act-ing like a hero and displaying physical courage is touched upon in *The Monument* as well, because Rafael realizes that his role as the gallant husband defending his wife during the meeting has en-hanced Mary's respect for him: "You are thinking of me as a hero. Oh, I know you, Mary, and I love the Mary I know, the hidden Mary, better than the one that is presented every day for my admira-tion. I love you because you are simple enough to love me for the incongruous things, because you want simplicity and convention in love as much as do all the other people of whom you make fun. I like being a hero very much. I like to be in the cinematic situation, admired for the braggadocio impulse" (p. 386). This is what Rafael thinks to himself after the scene, and in some way his heroic action is responsible for resolving the misunderstanding that has grown up between them and for bringing them together again.

In terms of subject matter *The Survival of the Fittest* is very closely linked to *The Monument*. Although the book covers a span of thirty years, more than half of it gives a picture of life as lived by a group of young Londoners in the 1930s. After the Second

World War the group disperses, and the last chapters are colored with a nostalgia for the past which makes it clear that the 1930s were the most formative period in the lives of the major characters.

The story centers around three people, Kit Mallings, Jo Upjohn, and Alison Petrie. All three of them are writers in their twenties when the novel opens. They have grown up in Clapham and move in the bohemian world of Chelsea and Bloomsbury—"Fitzrovia," as Alison calls it, after the Fitzroy Tavern, where they spent many evenings together. They spend their time talking about "politics and books and fame."[4] According to the "Author's Note" at the beginning of the book, both Kit and Alison are composite characters based on three separate sources. The sources that are most easily recognizable are Dylan Thomas in Kit, and the author herself in Alison. Alison is also strikingly like Mary Captor in *The Monument*. In fact the book that gave Mary Captor so much trouble in *The Monument* because of its unsavory subject, prostitution, is very similar to Alison's first novel which made her famous.

Kit is an ambitious and talented young writer who rises to fame. He is in love with Alison and introduces her to his best friend, Jo, who also falls in love with her. Alison is badly hurt by Kit, who is somewhat jealous of the extraordinary success of her first novel, and who does not hesitate to make fun of her "old-fashioned" morality in front of his friends. It doesn't take him long to fall in love with another girl, Polly, the daughter of a baronet, whom he marries. Alison finds solace in her friendship with Jo, but even though she sleeps with him on a single occasion she can never think of him as a future husband.

Jo is cast in the role of faithful friend to both Alison and Kit, for whom his love borders on the fringes of homosexuality. He is also the dutiful son and brother living with his ailing mother and looking after her when his sister leaves home to marry. In her highly appreciative review of this book Gerda Charles suggests that "it is the character of Jo which, standing at the center, holds (or should hold) the moral heart of the book in his hands." He stands for "such unfashionable virtues as endurance, acceptance, the settling, without screaming, for less; the not-so-bad-after-all."[5] Although she feels that the author does not succeed in giving him this status and misses the presence of genuine tragedy in the book, it would actually detract from the effect of creating a character like Jo if his fate were suddenly elevated to a tragic level. Jo suffers in silence, and the point of silent suffering is that it goes by unnoticed. That is its tragedy. Jo's mother, who has always complained of ill health, is still alive at the end of the book, while her son, who has hardly ever spoken of his illness, dies of leukemia.

Clement Maclaren and his wife, Georgina, also belong to the same circle as Kit, Alison, and Jo but are less important members of it. Clement is a journalist and his wife is an unconventionally promiscuous woman. Ironically enough, she feels shattered when her husband falls in love with a German refugee, Ilse. Clement divorces Georgina and marries Ilse, but she commits suicide in the mistaken belief that the Germans have invaded England. In the end Clement goes back to his wife, adopts her illegitimate son, Paul, and the two of them find happiness together.

Piers, Fay, and Davina are characters who enter the group through their involvement with the main figures. Piers is an army officer who has once been in love with Fay but has lost interest in her even before he meets and becomes fond of Alison. Alison and Piers marry and somewhat unexpectedly work out a remarkably successful marriage. Alison finds great satisfaction in her marriage, and as she grows older she writes less and less, seemingly content in her role as wife and mother.

Fay falls in love with Jo but he can never bring himself to ask her to marry him, partly because he is still in love with Alison and partly because he feels he cannot ask her to make a home with his mother. When Fay realizes that she has no future with Jo, she marries an army officer and enjoys the material comforts he offers her.

Davina is the daughter of the Labour M. P. who wins the elections in Jo's area after the war. Jo meets her a few years after Alison's marriage and they become engaged to be married. Suddenly Jo breaks off the engagement on the excuse of "ill health." Davina is very unhappy and tries hard to make him change his mind, but he remains inflexible. Ultimately Davina marries Kit, who has lost his first wife during the war. Kit is now a famous writer but an incurable alcoholic. He is invited to lecture in America and the Soviet Union, and dies after a bout of heavy drinking while traveling in the USSR with Jo as his only companion.

It is now time to clarify the elements that the three books have in common. The period of all three books is essentially the same. In *World's End* the events in the world at large, the civil war in Spain, the growth of socialism in England, and expressions of anti-Semitism are suggested through Brand's troubled thoughts about the events in history, and through the ideas of the Communist lodger, MacDonald, and Ma Hogben's reference to anti-Semitic feeling growing around them.

In *The Monument* all these subjects are present and assume even greater significance. Instead of a minor character like MacDonald, the Communist in *World's End*, two of the major characters, Mary Captor and Annie Sellars, are deeply committed to the Socialist cause. The book describes historic events like the General Strike, the demonstrations on May Day, the China campaign, and the signing of the treaty at Munich as part of the reality in which these fictional characters are involved. The question of anti-Semitic feeling is brought to the fore because Mary herself is married to a Jew, and also because one of Marcus Barradane's employees is an anti-Semite. When Marcus dismisses her, she attends one of the meetings where Mary is going to speak and heckles her, causing a riot. Mrs. Sellar's son is teased by his schoolmates because his mother takes part in demonstrations and marches and she tells him to say "that you're proud of your Ma because she wants to keep the Spanish children from being bombed and cruelly treated just as much as if they were her own" (p. 277). Mrs. Sellars's brand of socialism is not very revolutionary when it comes to her attitude toward Mary, however. On a visit to Mary's home she is full of naive admiration for her butler and all the outward splendor of Mary's way of life compared to her own. She expresses no resentment whatsoever, but seems rather to accept that Mary belongs to a different class (pp. 339–41).

Mary herself withdraws somewhat unexpectedly from her involvement in public affairs when she becomes pregnant. The voice of the narrator draws attention to this fact: "She has managed, by a process of self-hypnotism, to shutter the half of her mind; and with the other half she thinks only of herself and Rafael. The world flows serenely by her, not wetting even her feet. Sometimes she feels the harsher thought struggling to break through, but she is a match for it and with the opening of her eyes can drive it back into jail" (p. 417). It is strange to see Mary—the modern young woman who has written a shocking book about the life of a prostitute, who has demonstrated on May Day, who has been on the side of the laborers in the General Strike, and who has campaigned for the Socialists in Spain and in China—suddenly content to lead the life of a bourgeois housewife living in comfort in a flat in Hampstead, listening to music, giving parties, and doing nothing more actively philanthropic than getting her husband to donate his best Sisley to the National Gallery. However, the ending of the book suggests that this withdrawal is only temporary: "Mary closes the door, stands alone in the quiet hall. Oh, I will awaken, I promise you! For the present I am with my child in retreat, and for its sake am seeking my tower. For the present I am looking down from above on the earth foreshortened, am holding myself apart in the singing sky but I will descend!" (p. 420). The mention of the tower and the image of a person looking down from it recalls the persona of the narrator who stood on the tower at the beginning of the story. At the end the same voice intrudes and comments on the role of the artist in society: "This, then, is the beginning of a new day, a day that can never unfold till the poet come down from the tower to set his foot on the enemy earth that he has so long regarded through the reversing mirror, till he blow his pretentions off the back of his hand into the clouds from whence they came, until he beat his pen into a ploughshare" (p. 423). This passage is similar in content to the one giving Mary's thoughts as she looks on the life around her just a few pages earlier, and therefore suggests that she, who is a novelist, must take an active part in helping to change the society in which she lives.

In addition to having the same historical background the characters in *The Survival of the Fittest* are also politically involved. Jo is a member of the Labour party and Davina the daughter of the Labour member of Parliament. Kit and Jo fight with a fascist gang in the street and Ilse's plight is a grim reminder of the persecution of the Jews.

Unlike the other two novels, however, *The Survival of the Fittest* also includes the years of the war. The different ways in which the characters react to the bombs that begin to fall around them are described in a series of short scenes which flash from one to the other. Polly is terrified, Kit seems to be totally free of fear and sits writing during the raids, Georgina enjoys serving as a fire warden, and Alison spends the war years in Staines, waiting for her husband's return from the Middle East.

The Survival of the Fittest is also different from the other two novels in that it goes on to describe the years after the war and the birth of the next generation. The two parts are not equally balanced, however. The presentation of the children is very brief. James, Alison's eldest son, is the only one to play an important role as a link between the two generations. He forms a special friendship with Jo and is made Kit's literary executor when Jo dies. However, even James is seen primarily through the eyes of his mother, who is extremely proud of him, and his growth and development are reported in a few pages.

In his review of *The Survival of the Fittest* Robert Gorham Davies points out that "Miss Johnson makes no attempt, though her point of departure had seemed so political, to link the like experience of these two key generations."[6] It is a difficult task to try to cover the experience of two generations within a single volume and the outstanding impact of the novel is of the experience of the generation that grew up in the 1930s. This is why, in spite of its wider scope, it seems to belong with the novels that were written during that period itself, *World's End* and *The Monument*.

In addition to the fact that the main characters in all three novels have literary ambitions, many of the situations that occur in the personal life of the group of friends in *The Survival of the Fittest* are reminiscent of situations in *The Monument*. The way in which Jo Upjohn is tied by his sense of responsibility to his ailing mother is similar to the way in which Albert Whye is bound to his father in *The Monument*. One of the major causes of tension between Mary and Rafael in their marriage is the result of Rafael's desire to break away from his father and live independently. Mary tries to dissuade Rafael, feeling it will be unkind to Marcus. It takes her some time to see that Marcus blames her for trying to take Rafael away from him: "Strangling love, she thought. Rafael knew and I did not" (p. 259). She tells her father-in-law that she has been against the move and that she has since made up her mind to agree to it.

The pattern of Alison's life is also similar to Mary's in *The Monument*. Both of them fall in love with someone whom they find physically attractive and then marry a man who offers them comfort and security and with whom they find happiness on a realistic, down-to-earth level.

The way in which violence and tragedy enter the lives of ordinary people is also apparent in all three novels. In *World's End* Mr. Hogben commits suicide. In *The Monument* Bob Sellars is burned in a fire, Carel Constant is killed in an airplane crash, and Albert murders his father. In *The Survival of the Fittest* the man whom Jo's sister marries proves to have a streak of sexual perversity and commits suicide when he is arrested for pursuing a little girl in the park. Ilse is terrified of being caught by the Germans and commits suicide when she believes that they have landed in England. Polly and her daughter are both killed when a bomb lands on their home in the country. There is a cruel irony about both these deaths because the church bells that Ilse hears and interprets as a signal of the German invasion were rung by mistake, and Polly has left London because she felt the danger of being hit by a bomb was greater in the city than in the country. Violence and tragedy are seen to be lurking beneath the surface, as they were in the novels discussed in the previous chapter.

Narrative Technique

With regard to narrative technique *World's End* and *The Monument* have more in common than either does with *The Survival of the Fittest*. In the earlier two novels Johnson is still using the devices of the psychological novel whereas in the later book she has moved over to a more conventional type of third-person narrative. Thus even though all three books use the technique of parallel plots the episodes in *The Survival of the Fittest* are longer and more fully developed, and the impression of brief camera shots is not as pronounced as in the earlier books.

A device which she uses a great deal in *The Monument* links up with the analysis of technique in *This Bed Thy Centre* discussed in the previous chapter. The mirror is repeatedly used as a medium for revealing people. For example, Mary looks at herself in the mirror when she has begun to be aware of her feelings toward Rafael: "Mary looked in her mirror to be sure she was beautiful. Mirror, mirror on the wall, who is the fairest of us all?" (p. 160). Rafael also catches sight of his face in a mirror at a time of emotional disturbance: "Every thought etched into the lines of it. Very, very bright" (p. 198). On the night of their wedding "Rafael saw the slow blanching of her body among the shadows of his mirror. So is all happiness reflected, he thought, all beauty; was not Medusa so beautiful that no man could bear to look upon her secret face save in a shining shield? Here is the last treasure of my life's collecting, and I cannot see her completely for the distorting mirrors and shields of glory that stand between us" (p. 120). The need of a mirror through which to observe life is also suggested at the end of the book, when the narrator speaks of the poet looking at earth through a "reversing mirror." The various uses of the mirror are not integrated so as to make it into a symbol that has structural significance, but the repeated references to it suggest that it fascinates Johnson as a symbol for the novelist's art.

A noticeable difference between the style of the earlier and the later novels is the diminished use of the techniques of the psychological novel—the interior monologue and the stream-of-consciousness technique. In *World's End* Brand is constantly troubled about the state of the world; his inability to find a job, his infatuation for Rosemary, and his love for his wife. Doris worries about losing Brand to Rosemary, about their future together, and about the birth of her child. Their thoughts are recorded in a continuous flow in order to convey their internal state. Similarly, in *The Monument* there is a long interior monologue when Rafael roams the streets of Paris longing for Mary. His thoughts, as he watches Mary, are also constantly woven into the narrative of their lives together.

In *The Survival of the Fittest* the method of narration is less obtrusive. There is a more conventional third-person narrator and many pages of dialogue between the friends, whereas the use of interior monologue and stream of consciousness has virtually disappeared.

There is also a similar tuning down of the prose style. Whereas the earlier novels are full of poetic images, as for example in *The Monument*: "a new realisation grew into her thought like a paper blossoming under water" (p. 129), or lyrical descriptions like "The sun sets a tentative finger on the memorial of fire, on the tip of St. Paul's cross. The river whitens" (p. 423), the writing in *The Survival of the Fittest* is far less contrived. There are many passages of description, but in a style that is less consciously "literary." For example: "The sun came slantwise, gold as brandy, through the dark shimmer, and made a shifting pattern on the grass" (p. 394) is an excellent passage of description but it doesn't have any of the artificiality of syntax that is apparent in many of the poetic passages in the earlier novels. This is evidence of a greater sureness of touch in the later novels, where the style does not draw attention to itself but is perfectly suited to the subject. It reveals a consistent tendency on Johnson's part to move away from her early, more experimental style to a more sophisticated and subtle medium that is peculiarly her own.

Chapter Four

Two Minor Novels

Girdle of Venus (1939) and *The Family Pattern* (1942) belong to the small group of novels that are now out of print and unlikely to be reissued. Although neither of them can be considered to be a major novel they are of considerable interest because in them two basic tendencies in Pamela Hansford Johnson's fiction find extremely clear expression. In the novels already discussed it appears that the author was interested on the one hand in recording interior experience and on the other in dealing with the world outside and giving a panoramic view of society. These two tendencies find separate expression in these two novels. *Girdle of Venus* is essentially a psychological novel whereas *The Family Pattern* is a kind of historical chronicle.

Girdle of Venus

The main character in *Girdle of Venus* is a lonely middle-aged woman named Marcia Trapper. The story describes her effort to establish a new life for herself once all the people she has cared for are dead. She loses her only daughter when the girl is seven years old; her husband, Charley, dies after fifteen years of marriage spent happily in Clapham; and the book opens with the funeral of her brother-in-law. After the funeral she enters a pub and finds herself the center of attention when, on a casual impulse, she starts to read the palm of one of the women there. The incident foreshadows her future decision to become a fortune-teller. The title, *Girdle of*

Venus, is a reference to the palmist's vocabulary. She makes her decision by slow degrees. First she remembers an incident years ago when a palmist on the beach told her she had psychic powers, then she tells the fortune of her friend's fiancée as a joke. Finally when she visits this friend, Reg, and his wife, Betty, in their new home in the coastal town of Sandhampton, she finds the idea of settling there beside them attractive. By a remarkable coincidence the flat of the previous crystal-gazer proves to be vacant. The decision is made; she sets herself up as "Madame Marjanah" and wins a reputation for herself as a psychic. Gradually she realizes that she enjoys the feeling of power over people that her profession affords her. She becomes particularly involved in the affairs of a young girl, Katherine Ella Anderson. "Kella," as she is called, reminds her of her own dead daughter and Marcia's efforts to influence her life are an expression of her own frustrated needs as a mother. Kella consults Marcia because she cannot decide between two suitors, Herbert Ashley-Mayne, a well-established middle-aged businessman, and Harry Raikes, a poor young clerk who is deeply in love with her. Marcia encourages her to marry Herbert, and Kella becomes engaged to him.

In the meantime Marcia herself is falling in love with Frank Sword, a secretive and strong-minded middle-aged man who is rumored to have an insane wife. Frank is attracted to Marcia but he disapproves of her profession, and when she boasts of her ability to influence Kella's life he quarrels with her and stops seeing her. Soon after the quarrel Marcia finds that her own fortune has taken a turn for the worse. Mrs. MacCrossney, the hypochondriacal wife of the local doctor, commits suicide after Marcia has visited her and told her she has an incurable illness. Kella finds that she is unhappy in her engagement and unable to decide what to do. Many of Marcia's predictions are proved wrong. On the public level she has predicted that there will be no war, and on the private level she has told Betty that Reg, who is ill in the hospital, will live. When Reg dies, Betty confronts Marcia in a climactic scene, breaks her crystal, and reports Marcia to the police for practicing an illegal profession. In desperation Marcia turns to Frank and begs for his help. He insists that she should admit to Kella that she has never been able to see anything in her crystal ball. Upon learning this, Kella breaks off her engagement with Herbert and decides to remain unmarried for the time being. Marcia has to face the humiliation of being summoned to court and made to pay a fine. At their lowest ebb, her fortunes begin to rise again. She receives a letter of apology from Betty, she finds she has friends who are willing to defend her, and above all she regains Frank's friendship with the promise of love.

The story is lifted above the level of light fiction because of the moral significance attached to Marcia's decision as regards her profession. "Somewhere in the fourth dimension a battle was in progress between the white monsters and the black. Marcia watched it as calmly as if she had not been the prize. What a wreath I should make for the victor, she thought, a great fat woman bent backwards, looped head to heels to be set upon the forehead of the devil."[1]

In addition the psychology of a lonely woman is well grasped and conveyed. An imaginative person, the intensity of her thoughts often terrifies her. For example, when she hears that Frank is supposed to have been married to a woman who is shut up in an asylum, she is immediately overcome by horrid fancies: "As she stood there, fingers stuck out to touch the damp sill, black fear rose and rolled over her. Through it the circus passed, Charley in clown's suit balancing neatly on the crystal ball, the tenor groping with enormous banana hands for creatures that fled from him through the fog, the negro setting fire with a match to his own head so that it blazed like a pitch-pine torch, like a lyncher's torch in Alabama, and lastly, flying through the air, a mad girl screaming and shouting, waving her arms in sleeves a mile too long, sleeves that trailed away and away behind her" (p. 152). All the images put together in this paragraph are related to previous moments in Marcia's life, such as her brief encounter with an attractive tenor in the pub she visited after her brother-in-law's funeral. He walked her home through the fog and her imagination made him into such a threatening figure that the walk back to her mother-in-law's was full of inner terror. The nightmare quality of her thoughts is frequently recorded from her own point of view and succeeds in making the reader share her vision. Thus, for example, when she hears of the suicide of Mrs. MacCrossney she is overcome with fear of being held responsible for her death. A chance meeting with Doctor MacCrossney in the street takes on the quality of a nightmare:

She gasped for breath, tried to catch some of her courage as it flew. Watch the sea now, the sea spreading out under a mist; the moon rising. Far out on the waves a boat. A boat like a box.

Grinning in a silly way, Mrs. MacCrossney sat upright in the coffin.

Marcia could bear it no longer, the silence of the sea, the quiet horror of her thought. (pp. 269–70)

The psychology of her attraction to Kella and the way in which she makes Kella into a substitute for the child she has lost are also convincing and of sufficient interest to make her relationship with Kella into something more than a mere device of the plot.

As with the other novels already discussed, there are a few indications in this novel of a wider world outside the restricted one of the lives of the individuals described in the novel, but it is only referred to in passing. Frank, for example, is interested in world affairs and discusses the possibility of war breaking out. It is largely because of his conviction that there will be no war that Marcia Trapper confidently predicts peace to her clients. The topic of women's liberation is introduced through Betty, who speaks to Marcia of her disapproval of women fighting for the vote. Some of the interest in the problems of class-consciousness that was evident in the other books is also evident in the characterization of Marcia. She is proud of belonging to the respectable "middle class." She tries to console herself for the fact Charley came from the working class by remembering that "he had risen from Rotherhithe to Clapham Junction and come to have his own shop. His people were working-class, but there had been no need to see them often. Bess, had she lived, was to have gone to a private school" (p. 11). The fact that Marcia goes into a pub where most of the customers are working-class people and regards herself as their social superior is a reminder of the role class distinction plays in English life. All these wider concerns—the war, women's suffrage, and class-consciousness—are dealt with on a very superficial level in this novel. They are not related to the central subject, which is essentially the psychology of one rather eccentric and lonely woman.

The Family Pattern

The Family Pattern is the opposite of *Girdle of Venus* in that the lives of the family chosen as its subject are intimately connected to events in England. In a way the novel foreshadows *The Survival of the Fittest*, but the period that is chosen in *The Family Pattern* is 1891 to 1915, the years between the Boer War and the outbreak of the First World War.

The novel is divided into four parts of roughly equal length. The first part tells the story of the marriage between Mollie, a poor girl of humble origin, and Cosmo, a journalist several years her senior whose aim is to rise in the world. The difference between the background of the two parents is exemplified in their two daughters. Thomasine, the eldest, looks down upon her mother's relatives and is a conventional snob, whereas Melita loves them dearly and is a far more attractive personality. The marriage between their mother and father breaks up when Mollie discovers Cosmo has been unfaithful to her with a young actress named Shanon Glover. Even though Cosmo begs his wife's forgiveness she insists on a separation and obtains it. Cosmo and Shanon do not really care for each other and Shanon gives way to parental pressure and marries a knight, Sir George Ainslie. Their marriage is not a happy one and is brought to an abrupt end when Shanon dies onstage during a performance.

The second part of the novel describes the development of the two sisters. Thomasine marries the widower of her father's mistress, and after a time her father makes his home with her. Melita stays with her mother until her death. Soon afterwards she marries a poor working-class socialist named Johnny Stroud.

In Part Three the pattern of her mother's marriage is repeated to some extent in Thomasine's. After the birth of a son, Huon, Thomasine discovers that the passion between her and Sir George has faded and that he has been unfaithful to her. She decides to leave him but returns when she finds she is expecting another child. George and Thomasine lose their first child in a drowning accident, and George is obsessed with grief. Thomasine gives birth to another son, Charles, but she and her husband are completely estranged from each other. Melita, on the other hand, finds true happiness with her husband and shares his political ideals.

Part Four brings Thomasine's son and Melita's daughter, Iris, into the picture, and finishes the story of the two sisters' marriages. Thomasine discovers that her own father was the mysterious lover of her husband's first wife. George falls in love with the wife of one of his tenants, Connor James. Connor first sues for divorce and then commits suicide. His wife moves away to Brussels, and Thomasine is left trapped in her unhappy relationship with her husband. Melita also has to face tragedy. Her husband, who has always been against war, feels impelled to join up when England declares war and Melita's fear that he will be killed in action is realized. Left alone Melita chooses to go to live among her husband's people, the workers from whose midst her mother rose, and the family pattern is complete.

Closely interwoven with the personal story of the two sisters are the major issues of the period. Melita's marriage to Johnny brings her in touch with the working class and she finds that it is very difficult to win their acceptance. The way that she surmounts this obstacle reveals a great deal about the class-ridden structure of her society:

She was not going to commit the initial mistake of seeming different to her neighbours. Observing the kind of overalls the women wore in the mornings, she bought similar ones for herself, though she did take care to select those with the prettiest patterns.

The home that she made for Johnny had only a very subtle difference to the other homes in the row; but this subtlety was seized upon and noticed, and there were times during the first few months of marriage when she felt sick with panic. Could she live in this way, put aside all middle-class niceties, cut herself off entirely from her family? She wished Johnny had allowed her to go on working. It would have been good to go to town every day, to pretend things were as they had always been. She even found herself blaming Cosmo for his selfishness in consenting to the marriage, and one morning, when it came to her ears that she was, despite all her efforts, known in the row of houses as "Lady" Stroud, she broke down and cried with fear and desolation.[2]

The way in which Johnson describes Melita's struggle to be accepted by the neighborhood reveals the way in which class-distinction is deeply rooted in England. The workers despise the middle class as fiercely as the middle class despises them, and it is not easy to marry outside one's own class as Melita does. The contrast between the two sisters' way of life is a constant reminder of the ever-present problem of class in English society.

One of the minor characters in the novel, Melita's old schoolteacher Miss Carter, who has always been very fond of Melita, is a militant suffragette. She takes part in a suffragette rally and is badly knocked about, imprisoned, and forcibly fed. As a result of the treatment she receives in prison she dies. Melita's sympathy for her teacher's fate and her contact with her problem includes the struggle for universal suffrage within the framework of the events covered by the novel.

Johnny Stroud is an active Socialist. Melita joins the Labour party and the two of them become deeply involved with the political questions of their time. One of Johnny's severest moral decisions has to be taken when, in his capacity of strike leader, he has to take responsibility for organizing a strike at his brother-in-law's factory. Johnny has received employment there as a favor from his brother-in-law, but he decides to remain true to his political ideals and organizes the strike.

The first chapter in Part Three is entitled "England Changes" and sums up the values of the nineteenth century and the values of the middle class at that time: "The nineteenth century outlived its own lifetime, lingering as a ghost several years beyond the funeral. It should have died with the bell of the last midnight, or at least, with the death of the Queen; but it was the great century of the middle-class, and the middle-class was reluctant to face the ugly speeding of time, time that must inevitably blur the class outline, paint out the clear-cut edges and smooth them into the great, dangerous, unknown classes on either flank" (p. 149). In the same way other chapters describe the changes that take place in England at the beginning of the twentieth century—the defeat of the Lords, the passing of the bill for national health, and the stirrings of the coming war.

In this book more than in any of the previous novels Pamela Hansford Johnson shows the impact of history on the lives of individuals. In an interview with a Russian critic, V. V. Ivasheva, she says that she has always been interested in presenting contemporary man in the context of the time in which he lives. She feels that the lives of individuals are directly affected by world events and that they themselves are a part of world events.[3] *The Family Pattern* is the first book in which this interest in showing the relationship between individual lives and events in public affairs is brought to the fore. Perhaps the fact that the Second World War had broken out when *The Family Pattern* was written encouraged the novelist to delve into the past in an effort to find an explanation for the present. Not until she wrote *The Survival of the Fittest* some twenty years later did she try again to interweave private and public worlds to the same extent.

Chapter Five

The "Helena" Trilogy

Three of Pamela Hansford Johnson's novels, *Too Dear for My Possessing* (1940), *An Avenue of Stone* (1947), and *A Summer to Decide* (1948), have come to be known as the "Helena" trilogy. Even though she dies in the beginning of the third volume, Helena's influence is felt to be all-pervading and the author decided, in retrospect, to name the trilogy after her.[1] Although each volume is a self-contained unit, the entire trilogy can be read as the story of the development of the narrator, Claud Pickering, from the time of his thirteenth birthday until the time of his second marriage twenty-five years later. It is therefore possible to discuss the three volumes together.

A fourth volume, *Winter Quarters*, poses something of a problem. In it the three major characters of the trilogy make an appearance and some of the characters who are introduced are referred to in passing in subsequent volumes of the trilogy. In terms of chronology it comes directly after *Too Dear for My Possessing* and deals with the period covered by the Second World War. In spite of these links with the trilogy, the main subject of *Winter Quarters* and its method of narration are completely different. The differences are, in fact, more important than the similarities. The book has not been reissued and is now so rare that even the author no longer has a copy (*Avenue*, p. 5). To deal with it where it belongs chronologically would seriously interfere with the unity of the trilogy, and it seems best to look at it in a section by itself at the beginning of this chapter.

Winter Quarters

Winter Quarters is more closely related to Johnson's earlier novels than to the trilogy and the novels that came after. In it she continues to use a contrapuntal technique to reveal the lives of several people arbitrarily linked togther. In a prefatory note the author says her aim is "to explore the reactions of 'ordinary' men to an 'extraordinary' way of living."[2] She chooses to capture the lives of the men in an English artillery battery during a period of five days spent waiting for orders in a small English village before the Eighth Army launched its offensive in Egypt during the Second World War. One of the second lieutenants, Eric Cassilis, sums up the situation: "Look at this Battery. Only a handful of men have ever seen active service. They're taken from their homes and planted down in alien corn—not to act, not to relieve the strangeness by action, but to wait indefinitely for God knows what. To go to all the bother of establishing a temporary world. And to make matters more complicated, they're stuck among people to whom this village world is permanent, and though they can't destroy it for them, they can shake it till the surface crumbles away" (p. 11). This interaction between the men in the battery and the people in the village is shown by dividing the characters into the categories of "soldiers" and "civilians" and then exposing them in a series of scenes that take place in the camp, in the sergeant's mess, and in the local pub over a period of five days.

During these scenes the background and present involvements of a great many different people are revealed. Among the soldiers, a gunner, Victor Tawney, emerges as an important character. A lazy but charming young aristocrat, he secretly feels disgraced for not having become an officer. He drifts into an involvement with the pub landlord's flirtatious wife, Gillian Eagles. One of the local village girls, Eileen Fogg, nurses a secret passion for him and brings a great deal of trouble on his head by telling her aunt that he is the father of the baby she mistakenly believes herself to be expecting. Another one of the soldiers whose personal life becomes complicated is Sergeant Menhenheott, who finds his true love, Phyllis, while he is stationed in the village and has to face the unpleasant task of breaking a previous engagement with a predatory young woman back home. A happy marriage is also included in the many relationships revealed in the novel. Lieutenant Strutt and his wife, Stacey, are an exemplary couple. She comes to visit him and tells him the exciting news that they are expecting a child. Her happiness is reflected in her delight in everything around her and by the author's entering into her mind and recording her thoughts.

Sam Eagles and his wife, Gillian, are the center of a great deal of interest because they own the local pub, the Golden Fleece, where everybody gathers and where quite a few scenes are enacted. Sam is several years older than his wife and extremely jealous of her relationship with several of the men in the battery. Gillian encourages the attentions of the men around her and has sent away her two-year-old son so as to be free to enjoy herself. Eventually she and her husband are reconciled and she returns to the role of wife and mother.

A young poet, Tom Berry; an overprotected widow's son, Chris Dakin; an Englishman of the old-school type, Ives Elvorden; and an unhappily married young man, Bert Lilley, are minor characters who help to give the impression of a battery of soldiers from widely differing backgrounds who would probably never have come together but for the contingency of war.

Among all these characters, the part played by the three main characters in the trilogy is comparatively small. Claud Pickering is the battery captain whose personal life is uneventful during the period covered by this novel. His previous life as revealed in *Too Dear for My Possessing* is rapidly summarized when he appears. His artistic sensibility is made evident in the way he looks at the village: "small and square in the richness of autumn, the rough-cast cottages catching brilliance from the sun, the orange rooftops drawing from it some appearance of textural change, as if the bricks might yield like gingerbread to the pressure of a finger" (p. 14). Like the art critic that he is in civilian life, he thinks of the scene as if it could have been painted by Bonnard. Otherwise his general reaction to his situation in *Winter Quarters* is summed up in his thought that: "the most remarkable thing about this war is that I have become a soldier at all" (p. 15). Pickering's half-sister, Charmain, comes to visit him and attends the dance that the soldiers organize to help them pass the time waiting. She has been disappointed in love and needs a change. She becomes friends with Victor Tawney, but in one of the subsequent volumes of the trilogy we learn that Tawney was killed in action. In *Winter Quarters*, Pickering is hit by a splinter from a bomb and taken to the hospital. There he is visited by both Charmain and his stepmother, Helena, who remains true to the picture of her that is created in *Too Dear for My Possessing*. Apart from showing that Pickering was involved in the war, *Winter Quarters* does not add much to the knowledge of Claud and his family that is gained from the trilogy.

Most of the critics who reviewed *Winter Quarters* commented upon the remarkable fact that a woman writer should try to describe the life of men in an army camp. Isabelle Mallet feels that Johnson fails to show "how men behave when they are being manly together."[3] Three male critics, however, maintain that she has achieved a considerable measure of success.[4] Pamela Hansford Johnson is not really trying to show "men being manly together." She is far more concerned with creating a realistic picture of a small community in a way that recalls her purpose in *This Bed Thy Centre* and *Here Today*. The emphasis of the book is upon the human aspect of these people's existence. *Winter Quarters* also resembles the earlier books in the use the author makes of stream of consciousness and of the "Huxleyan" technique of counterpoint to reveal the minds and feelings of a large variety of people who have been brought together.

The "Helena" Trilogy

In tracing the development of Pamela Hansford Johnson's art, Isabel Quigly suggests that the five novels that followed *This Bed Thy Centre* did not really fulfill its promise and that it was with the appearance of *Too Dear for My Possessing* that "her gifts seemed to fall into place, her style to take the right direction."[5] She also maintains that taken as a whole the trilogy is probably Johnson's "most impressive achievement."[6] Recently, the reissue of all three volumes of the trilogy is an additional indication of the central place these three novels occupy in her work.

Each one of these three books has been singled out for special praise by different critics. When *Too Dear for My Possessing* appeared it was hailed as a "new work by a brilliant writer" and described as "a book of queer enchantment; of strange astringent realism; a book stripped utterly of sentimentality but deep with feeling that is both psychic and sensuous."[7] In a long article on Johnson's work the critic in the *Times Literary Supplement* claims that *"An Avenue of Stone* lies at the centre of all Miss Hansford Johnson's "fiction" and regards it as the "centrepiece" of the trilogy.[8] Writing on the reissue of the trilogy a few years ago Anne Duchêne maintained that *A Summer to Decide* "is much the best of that sequence."[9] Thus each volume has found its votary and it is probably fair to conclude that all three are successful in upholding a common standard and attaining a unity of tone.

The narrator of all three books in the trilogy is Claud Pickering. In *Too Dear for My Possessing* he sits down as a mature man in his thirties to tell the story of his youthful experience of falling in love with a dream. In *An Avenue of Stone* he relates the story of his step-mother's desperate last bid for love, and in *A Summer to Decide* he tells of his half-sister's painful decision to remain married to a man whom she no longer loves and his own decision to marry for a second time.

Too Dear for My Possessing

Too Dear for My Possessing takes its title from a Shakespearian sonnet which is quoted in full on the title page. The beloved to whom the narrator is thus bidding farewell is Cecil Archer, who epitomizes his romantic dream. At the end of the novel it is clear that he has set himself the task of writing the story down as a way of coming to terms with reality.

The book is divided into four carefully balanced parts, each with exactly four chapters. The setting changes from Bruges, where

Claud spent his childhood, to London where he was educated and grew up, to Paris where he spent the important years of his first marriage, and finally back to Bruges where he returns after an absence of eighteen years to come to terms with his experience.

Although the emphasis of the book is upon Claud's inner life and his relationships with people, there is also a conventional story which is gradually unfolded. Claud's father, Richard Pickering, falls in love with an Irish singer, Helena Shea, when his son is ten years old. Unable to obtain a divorce, he leaves England for Bruges taking his mistress and his son with him. When he is thirteen, Claud's mother, Lallah, comes to visit her son, accompanied by her newly acquired friend Daniel Archer and his daughter Cecil, then only twelve. Cecil awakens Claud's dormant sexuality but circumstances work against their relationship developing. Cecil returns to England with her father and makes a career for herself as an actress in musical comedy. Claud's mother dies, his father marries Helena, and soon afterwards he is sent to his maternal uncle in England, where he completes his education. During his first year there his father also dies and Helena decides to return to England. Claud chooses to live with Helena and his newly born half-sister: they set up house together in Battersea.

During the years that follow Claud is often reminded of Cecil, who rapidly rises to fame as a star in musical comedy. Claud is afraid of meeting her because he feels she has moved out of his reach. Instead he meets and falls in love with a pleasant young girl at his office, marries her in spite of Helena's forebodings, and moves to Paris. It does not take long for the marriage to prove a failure. Ultimately Claud seeks Cecil out and enjoys a brief moment of perfect happiness with her in the acknowledgment of mutual love. Once more, circumstances force them apart. Claud cannot desert his wife, and Cecil continues to pursue her career. By an irony of fate it is only after Cecil's death, while on tour in America, that Claud is left free. His wife, Meg, has fallen in love with another man and Claud offers her a divorce. He retreats to the place of his childhood and faces the fact that all through the years that have passed he has been in love with a dream.

The effect of setting the action of *Too Dear for My Possessing* entirely in the past is the creation of a situation whereby the way in which memory functions becomes extremely important. Isabel Quigly has already noted the influence of Proust on this book.[10] This influence is apparent in the way Claud sets out as a mature man to try to recapture the past. Throughout the book there are passages which highlight the significance of the way in which the mind stores details in the memory. When Claud has to leave his beloved city, Bruges, for London he walks around the city trying to store up memories of his happy days there: "I was grateful for the knowledge that the memories I stored were whole and living, that they would not decay, that the city would fall before they fell, and that they should stand forth above its dust" (p. 83). He also emphasizes the way memory encapsulates seemingly unimportant incidents: "It is an odd thing, memory, and odd how often it will retain things of no importance. Memory has no more discrimination than a jackdaw; it fills the caverns of the mind with rubbish and gold—diamonds and glass. Sometimes it adds to the storehouse something not its own, not of memory, but of the mind's new creating" (p. 85). On many occasions in the book the truth of this reflection is demonstrated. Claud leaving Bruges and saying good-bye to his father, remembers a water-drop glinting on the cheek of a nun, and his father waving a yellow silk handkerchief (p. 85). On another occasion, at a party just before Cecil enters, he sees his friend, Philip Crandell, wearing a raspberry silk tie: "Turn the lock on it, memory, on Crandell's tie; for it was the herald of her coming, her torchlight, her preceding flame" (p. 158).

The image of the lock and key is used several times in the novel and sets up reverberations of its own in the text: for example, when Claud meets Cecil in Paris he tells her, "We've got to isolate this, Darling Cecy, put it away in a box and turn the key on it" (p. 252). At the end of the book when Claud returns to Bruges after an absence of eighteen years he takes his half-sister with him. When she asks him to take her to see "Villa Moustique" he feels as "though a golden key had fallen from heaven into my hand, a key with which I could unlock the safe in which were hidden the answers to all questions" (p. 313). The journey they make in the boat recalls the journey he had imagined himself making with Cecil. He asks Charmian to sing Cecil's theme song and is so much absorbed in the past that he even calls Charmian "Cecy." But the effort to recreate the past is not wholly successful. The waterway leading to the villa is quite impenetrable and Claud realizes that he does not really want to see it again. After this experience he is able to dedicate his book to Cecil and accept the fact that she is only a memory:

How fortunate we are that the past is inviolable and that it is our right to preserve what we will of it! Not that we can re-create old happiness to the touch and the vision. A pebble we shut in a box three score years ago will have changed when we take it out again; surely it was bigger, redder, more shining? It must have been a beautiful stone or we should not have guarded it so jealously; but now—O look! it has lost its splendour. It is best to turn the key on the box and drop the box and key into the river, for then the alchemy of memory will turn the stone to gold. . . . Because I left my villa to stand or fall as it would, it stands yet; and her image dances in the dusty mirror, and from the upper windows she can still be seen in the boat where she sits waiting. (pp. 318–19)

This passage makes it clear that in the process of retelling the story of his unfulfilled love for Cecil, Claud has created something new and different from the original experience because it has been processed by the "alchemy of memory."

In both *An Avenue of Stone* and *A Summer to Decide* the theme of memory is omitted from the novels because in these two books Claud is describing events as they happen and not remembering something that happened a long time ago. These novels continue the story of Claud's relationship with Helena and Charmian, the two women who dominate his thoughts once he has divorced his first wife. The story in *An Avenue of Stone* focuses on Helena's love affair with John Field, and on Charmian's unhappy marriage. Claud plays the part of an observer, who cares very deeply for the people involved but who has to learn to accept a passive role.

An Avenue of Stone

At the beginning of *An Avenue of Stone* Helena is left a widow once more. The book tells of her struggle to face loneliness and old age. The title is explained in a paragraph that describes Helena's experience of old age: "Those who have lived richly, exhaustively, staring into every face, attentive to every voice, are only too often pursued by the spinster Furies, and are driven at the end down avenues of stone where the walls reach to the sky, and the doors are sealed, and the pavements are rubbered against all sound but the beat of the hurrying heart" (p. 249). The "avenue of stone" down which Helena is driven is fruitless love.

An Avenue of Stone is divided into four equally balanced parts. The first part shows how John Field, a weak young man of Claud's age who had served as a subaltern in Claud's battery in Africa during the Second World War, meets Claud and comes to live as a lodger in Helena's home. The second part shows the development of Helena's passion for Johnny and his weak submission to her dominance. In the third part, he leaves her for another lonely widow, Mrs. Olney, a woman from Daniel Archer's past who has taken advantage of Helena's generosity and friendship to win Johnny's affection for herself. The fourth part shows John Field's liberation from both these lonely older women and the growth of his love for Naomi, a woman of his own age whom he marries without giving Helena fair warning of the shock his marriage will be to her.

In an article on Pamela Hansford Johnson, a critic suggests that the theme of *An Avenue of Stone* is "the betrayal of the first-rate or the good in heart by the warped, the hangers-on or the discomfited."[11] Johnny Field is one of these "hangers-on," a man who hurts Helena because he is too weak to tell her that he is not in love with her. In a crucial scene Claud overhears Johnny boasting of Helena's infatuation for him to a girl he meets in the pub (p. 170). As the critic in the *Times Literary Supplement* points out, this "is like one of the great moral 'recognition' scenes in the later James."[12]

A minor thread in the story is the description of Charmian's marriage to Evan Sholto. Claud tells of his belief that Charmian could have fallen in love with Victor Tawney, a gunner in his battery, except for the fact that he was killed at Alamein before a romance could develop between them. He instinctively dislikes her husband, Evan Sholto, "a handsome, weak-eyed, oldish young man with a curious fetish of helplessness" (p. 20). Helena also dislikes Evan and his subsequent behavior justifies both Claud and Helena's dislike. In *An Avenue of Stone* he is unfaithful to Charmian, but because she is still in love with him she forgives him. In *A Summer to Decide* he becomes involved in shady business and is imprisoned. By another Jamesian irony, the money that her stepfather left Charmian instead of Helena becomes her prison because she realizes that she can use her wealth to help Sholto to live well and regain his self-respect. As Claud observes in *A Summer to Decide*, "Daniel could not have done her a worse turn than to leave her a sum sufficient to preclude endeavour and to cement the parasite forever to her hearth."[13]

A Summer to Decide

A Summer to Decide continues the story of *An Avenue of Stone* almost without a break. This novel is divided into three parts, each of which have seven chapters, but the story is not as neatly structured as the story of Helena's love for John Field in the previous book. Instead, in the third volume of the trilogy, Pamela Hansford Johnson returns to her earlier interest in tracing the lives of several people at once and the narrative focuses alternately on Charmian's marriage; on John Field and Naomi, the girl he married at the end of *An Avenue of Stone*; on Helena's death; and on Claud's relationship with two women who enter his life—Harriet Chandler and Ellen Ashton. The story progresses very slowly because the emphasis is on character rather than incident.

Charmian's situation in the third book is very much the same as it was in *An Avenue of Stone* except that she has become a mother and her love for Evan has abated. Claud tries hard to persuade her to break away from her husband and his insistence causes a breach between them. Eventually Claud is "convinced that Charmian was a better human being than myself in every conceivable way, that she had more compassion and in a sense more wisdom, but that she would sink where I should swim, would be hauled down inevitably by the clambering arms of the useless and the dead, who believed that they were valuable and alive" (p. 95). The course of events shows that Claud's judgment is correct. Evan Sholto takes the risk of making quick money by selling stolen cars and is caught when one of the workers at the garage reports him. John Field is also involved in the business with Evan and is selling secret information to the press as well. After both young men have been tried and served their sentences they return to their wives. Naomi and John have weathered the crisis well and their love for each other is stronger than ever. Charmian is determined to stand by Evan, but he takes to drink and there is no hope of a renewal of affection between the two of them. One of the strengths of this novel is the author's refusal to compromise and make things easier for Charmian. The situation of a strong young woman like Charmian who stands by her decision to marry a man long after she has ceased to love him is common enough in real life, but seldom explored in depth in fiction. It becomes a theme that Johnson returns to several times in her later work.

Claud is luckier than his sister. He finds a woman who is able to offer him a more mature and down-to-earth love than his early passion for Cecil. He meets a young widow, Ellen Ashton, through John and Naomi Field and is immediately attracted to her. Charmian and Ellen become good friends, but it takes Claud a long time to commit himself to her. He is also attracted by a completely different kind of woman, Harriet Chandler, the cousin of his friend Philip Crandell. Harriet is a glamorous and progressive young woman who is visiting England but settled in America. When Crandell offers Claud, who is working in his gallery, the chance of going to America to acquire some paintings, Claud welcomes it. He meets Hattie unexpectedly on the boat and accepts her invitation to visit her in New York. While in America he is disappointed when he receives a cold and impersonal letter from Ellen and takes

his revenge on her by spending a lot of time with Harriet and hint-
ing of the possibility of marrying her in his reply to Ellen's letter.
Ellen is so hurt by his behavior that it takes her a long time to agree
to marry him when he finally brings himself to make the proposal.
She insists on Claud's accepting a secure position as the curator of
a museum as a test of his willingness to take the responsibility of
marriage seriously enough. The gradual shifts of mood and the
difficulties that present themselves in the process of their working
out a satisfactory relationship are minutely traced and make the
interest of this novel primarily psychological.

Claud and Helena

Claud's relationship with Helena is worth detailed analysis because it dominates his thoughts in all three books of the trilogy.
Lisle Bell points out that in *Too Dear for My Possessing* the love
story "is fragile and dreamlike, untested by realities. What gives the
novel its vitality and its undeniable impact on the imagination is
quite a different element—the strength of a bond between a boy of
thirteen and his father's mistress. In tracing the relationship, part
enemy and part a shared affection, through the years that followed, Miss Johnson handles difficult material with assurance and
subtle shading."[14]
Pamela Hansford Johnson has commented on the relationship
herself in the preface to the second edition of *An Avenue of Stone*:
"The situation of Claud and Helena is a peculiar one. First he hates
his step-mother; then he comes to tolerate her; then, in an unsenti-
mental way, to love her. She is not an octopus woman at all, but
while she lives she is inevitably in the forefront of his thoughts"
(p. 5). Actually Claud does not ever express unadulterated hatred
for Helena, not even at the beginning of the first book. He finds
Helena crude and calculating and realizes that she resents his
presence. He is afraid of her temper but at the same time he is aware
of her beauty. The ambivalence of the emotions she arouses in him
is clearly expressed in the scene where Claud runs away from her
down to the quayside where his friends are waiting to accompany

him on an excursion in his boat. Helena forbids Claud to go as a punishment for having ruined the carpet in his room with his paints. Since she has previously promised him a picnic basket which is lying ready for him he picks it up and runs away with Helena in angry pursuit: "I can see her now, running over the cobbles in her apron and red slippers, a splendid fury whose face was black with blood under a burning brazier of hair. She shouted as she ran and waved her arms, called me sneak, runt, little rat, and even as I pulled the boat out into the square of dark water I could not help but think how horrible and fine she was" (p. 57). The words "horrible and fine" express the ambivalence of his feelings towards her even then. Later, when he is enjoying the picnic she had packed for him, he thinks: "How good Helena could be while the rich impulse was upon her! She was two people in one" (p. 59).

Once Claud is sent away to England to the middle-class respectability of his Uncle James's home in Hampstead, he finds himself longing to see Helena: "I had forgotten the things I detested in her, her spite, her sudden savagery. Defiantly my mind resisted Uncle James's tacit disapproval of her, Maud's censure freely expressed on every visit. Helena had sung *Annie Laurie* had sung it right there in the kitchen to make me laugh, and whenever I laughed with her, ephemeral sympathy sprang up between us. I had quite forgotten that immediately following this entertainment she had sent me upstairs to hear Father's suggestion that I be sent to England. Sometimes I hungered for her as I hungered for rich foods certain to make me sick" (p. 96).

After his father's death and Helena's arrival in England, Claud realizes that his relationship with her has undergone a subtle change: "In some way she was dependent upon me, often eager to ask my advice; it was as though my separation from her had snapped the leading strings" (p. 119). The relationship that develops between the passionate and beautiful stepmother and her stepson affects his ability to form a successful relationship with young women of his own age. Johnson has suggested as much in a telling parenthesis: "It is not altogether without Freudian significance, I suppose, that Claud eventually marries a girl called Ellen

(*Avenue*, 2nd. ed., p. 5). An early example of the effect of his knowledge of the passionate love between his father and Helena is the way he reacts when one of his first girl friends tries to elicit a kiss from him: "I saw the girl Meg on the parade, saw my mother and Archer, saw Helena and my father; and I said furiously, 'Well, I don't like it'" (p. 126). All the people mentioned in this quotation are associated with sexuality. Meg is a young woman of easy virtue, Claud's mother is attracted by Daniel Archer when she comes to visit her teenage son, and Helena lives as Claud's father's mistress for several years before she marries him.

Years later, Claud's inability to establish contact with Cecil is also linked to his relationship with Helena. After much delay Claud has just brought himself to the point of buying tickets for a performance of a play in which Cecil is acting, *The Honey Pot*. The night before he is due to go there he discovers that Helena is sleeping with the lodger she has taken in. Claud is so furious that he strikes Helena and forces her to agree to get rid of her lover. In some obscure way he blames Helena for his subsequent decision not to go to the theater the next day: "She made me drive Cecil off, and without generosity had ripped away my last faint delusion that she herself was content to take me and Charmian into her love without further desire" (p. 137).

Even so, it is Helena who is responsible for Claud's decision to go to Cecil in Paris. When Helena visits Claud she realizes that he is not happy with his wife and tells him that Cecil is going to perform in a cabaret in Paris. As if in a dream Claud goes to wait outside the theater and when Cecil appears the two of them are instantly drawn together in mutual recognition. Cecil is then closely associated with Helena. When Claud tells Cecil that he has been starving for her (p. 247), he recalls that these are exactly the words he has previously used to tell his wife how he feels about Helena (p. 224). When he spends the night in a hotel with Cecil he feels he is repeating the pattern of his father's life with Helena: "For a moment I was flooded with dread. 'Like Father,' I said, 'and Helena.' 'Like my father,' said Cecil softly, 'and Mrs. This and Mrs. That, No, darling, like none of them; like us'" (p. 248).

In the second book of the trilogy, *An Avenue of Stone*, Claud
has achieved a perspective on his relationship with Helena and is
able to analyze his feelings very clearly:

I have always recognized a tormenting emotion that lies between friendship and love; something stronger than the first and less demanding
than the second, though it may well exceed it in endurance. It may
exist between man and man, or between woman and woman, but as
it has some undefined sexual element, it exists more frequently between
man and woman. It is a torment of understanding that can have no
physical expression. For a lifetime it may remain unexpressed; if it
seeks the normal expression of love it is ruined. It is, if one must give
a name to it, the highest form of friendship, and is mysterious in origin.
Two persons of complete diversity, socially, physically, intellectually,
may feel it for each other. Each may be partnered in complete happiness
by another person; but were he to lose the friend with whom he shares
this third emotion his life would lose, irretrievably, a shade of colour,
a degree of light. It is the very fret that keeps the emotion alive; as if
both friends were seeking for an unnamed symbol lying between A and
B, a vital force mysteriously unrecognized by science or by literature.
Helena, but for five years, was twice my age. To say I loved her would
have been an embarrassing absurdity. To say that we were friends would
have been a foolish understatement. Endearments, even of the slightest
nature, never passed between us, unless you count the scrape of a kiss
at partings or reunions; yet I felt that at my life's end I should know
a sense of utter frustration that I had never been able to express in
some physical fashion, or by some new form of words, the love I had
for her. I am driven back even now on the terms "friendship," "love":
on A and B. Neither will do. (pp. 28–29)

This complex mixture between love and friendship that Claud is
attempting to describe runs as a strong undercurrent to the main
narrative in *An Avenue of Stone* and *A Summer to Decide* and is
the reason why the trilogy is named after Helena. When Helena
finally dies at the beginning of *A Summer to Decide* it takes Claud
a long time to recover from his sense of guilt and grief. The incidents are carefully arranged so as to delay Claud's arrival at the
hospital until after Helena's death. Claud has to overcome his

enormous sense of guilt for having left her to die alone. Once he begins to recover from the trauma of grief he begins to feel a sense of relief (p. 47). Even so his thoughts go back to Helena on many occasions and it is not until he has quarreled with John Field and recognized the truth of his claim that Helena was also responsible for some of the unhappiness he caused her that Claud is finally free of Helena's spell (p. 313). At the end of the trilogy he faces up to the responsibility of a mature relationship in marriage and starts life afresh with his second wife, Ellen Ashton. The fact that Ellen reminds Claud of both his first romantic love, Cecil, and of his step-mother is made explicit in *A Summer to Decide*. When he shows Naomi an etching of Cecil that was made by his friend Brickland, Naomi says it resembles Ellen (p. 124). Later, when Ellen is discussing her name—"Mine is simply a version of Helen; Helena, Ellen, Ella, Eleanor—they're all the same"—he finds that he is disturbed by what she has said. Soon afterwards he realizes why he has been troubled: "How far had her very name attracted me to her in the first place? In women, was I looking not only for Cecil but for Helena also? I began to believe that despite obvious dissimilarities, there was something in common between Helena's nature and Ellen's" (p. 154).

Common Features of the Trilogy

A minor character type that is repeatedly introduced in all three books of the trilogy is the possessive and demanding parent. In *Too Dear for My Possessing* the mother of Claud's first wife, Meg, creates a lot of tension between Claud and his wife. She tries to influence Meg even after her marriage, and when Claud discovers that Mrs. Ettrick has encouraged Meg to conceal from him the fact that she cannot have a baby he makes a dramatic break with his mother-in-law and refuses to see her again (p. 218). In *An Avenue of Stone*, Mrs. Sholto is an overpossessive, overindulgent mother who is largely to blame for her son's weakness. In *A Summer to Decide* the fact that Mrs. Sholto lives with Charmian and Evan is a constant burden on Charmian. In the end Charmian's only assertion of independence is expressed in her insistence that she will no longer live with Mrs. Sholto. The problem solves itself soon after because Mrs. Sholto dies, but the portrait of her in the novel is that of an extremely unsympathetic woman. In the last book of the trilogy, the girl with whom Claud falls in love, Ellen, is handicapped by the fact that she has an ailing and aged father. Stephen Copeland does all he can to show how much he resents Ellen's leaving him and in the end he refuses to attend his daughter's marriage to Claud. This character-type has already been introduced in several of the earlier novels and is evidence of the author's enduring interest in it.

In all three books the author has tried to introduce world events. In *Too Dear for My Possessing* Claud has a very minor interest in politics. Marianne Hauser points out that "in between the plot are squeezed, rather inorganically, the brief political statements, which are on the must-list of most contemporary novelists: Dollfuss firing at the socialists; Hitler ruling Germany; the Spanish war."[15] It is true that the references to politics contained in the first book are not required by the main theme of the novel and Claud's comments on politics are very cursory indeed: "Politics for the first time, began to interest me. I had the leisure for them and the mind for learning. When the Spanish War broke out I supported the Madrid Government giving my name to manifestoes and appeals, sitting on Medical Aid committees" (p. 298). However, he admits that his interest is purely intellectual: "I read, I argued, I grew tired; that was all" (p. 298).

On the other hand in commenting on the "wartime trilogy" A. S. Byatt observes that "Pamela Hansford Johnson created in precise detail a whole world of black market, shell shock, rationing, requisitioning, button-polishing."[16] It is certainly true that the impression of what it was like to live in postwar London is very strongly conveyed in both *An Avenue of Stone* and *A Summer to Decide*. In *An Avenue of Stone* Helena introduces Claud as a Socialist and speaks about her class's being doomed by the war (Claud enjoys the irony of seeing Helena, the pub singer, airing herself as "Lady Archer" in front of Mrs. Sholto and her friends). There are also several references to the way in which Daniel and Helena have lived on black-market goods during the war and the way in which they have reacted to the bombs. Daniel was terrified, like Polly in *The Survival of the Fittest*, and Helena simply incapable of understanding his fear, like Kit in the same book. A long chapter describes Charmian and Claud's reactions on V-Day with a discussion of their feelings about the war. There is a detailed description of postwar London with its bombed sites in *A Summer to Decide* and when Claud visits America the comparative luxury of life there is a striking contrast to the hardships of postwar London. Claud sums up the impact of the war in *A Summer to Decide*: "The war had made for all of us a declaration of age. Had it never occurred, I think we might have passed easily enough from youth into our middle years, but this gap, this dispersal, had brought us all to a halt, and we were slow to move on again" (p. 50).

In all three books of the trilogy Claud's sensibility is the filter through which events and relationships are viewed and interpreted. In her review of *Too Dear for My Possessing*, Janet Adam Smith feels that there is a tendency to wallow in Claud's sensibility and she doubts whether it is enough to carry the weight of an entire novel. Desmond Hawkins also complains of a "portentousness of address" that creates a disturbing undercurrent throughout the novel.[17] In the first volume of the trilogy Claud is established as a sensitive and imaginative young boy. His love of painting is expressed on the very first page of *Too Dear for My Possessing* when he describes his delight in his father's company and the way they visited the museums in Belgium together. The paintbox that his mother gives him as a birthday present is his passport to the creative world of the artist and he describes the joy that it gives him to paint. Claud's interest in art and literature is developed at school, where he wins a prize with an essay written on Flemish painting and matriculates with an essay on the history of painting. One of his best friends at school becomes a famous artist and advises Claud to become an art critic. Even though Claud first finds work in a bank, he writes a great many articles on painting and is overjoyed when one of his friends, Philip Crandell, starts a magazine and offers him the job of an art critic. The review of the "Tilford and Essen" show marks a milestone in his career.

In *An Avenue of Stone* he moves in a circle of literary men and artists. One of his friends, Swain, is an excellent painter: "He was profoundly interested in men and women, in the work they did and the worlds in which they moved; he painted them not as the components of a design, but as thinking and breathing beings, their fears and anxieties dark as night behind their eyes, and their hopes brilliant as day" (p. 185). In all three books there is a constant reminder of Claud's interest in art. In *A Summer to Decide* he works in a gallery with a friend and settles down as the curator of a small museum where he will take care of a large donation of paintings.

It is therefore very natural for Claud to describe scenes and people in visual terms or with reference to the works of great painters. Helena, for example, "was a Rubens woman, as big, as healthy, as full of radiant light and heat" (*Too Dear*, p. 110). On other occasions she is compared to a Veronese or to a Moyses Stevens flower piece. His aunt Maud "had dark hair that she tinted with tea leaves whenever it showed signs of greyness, so producing a Rembrandtesque effect of night and sunset at the point of fusion" (*Too Dear*, p. 89). Paris is described as a painter would see it: "Before me Paris lay blue and cold and lovely, a queen garlanded with mist. Low-lying clouds of frost and faint blue fog rolled in the great basin; and out of them grew spires and towers and long chimneys like the fingers of drowning men clutching upwards at the sunstraws of the morning" (*Too Dear*, p. 209). Descriptions such as these reflect a happy merging of Pamela Hansford Johnson's love of painting and the fictional narrator's perception.

Claud not only has the artist's eye, but he has the artist's sensitivity as well. His sensitivity as a child is well conveyed in descriptions of his awareness of moods and emotions and the intensity with which he experiences joy, despair, and guilt. Sitting in his boat full of happiness, he realizes that "if I stay here any longer I shall spoil everything. If I use up all this joy at one time, I shall have no reserve when most I need it" (p. 19). When he returns home late he finds out that his father is ill, and, in the way of the sensitive child, he immediately sees it as an act of retribution: "Was it such a dreadful thing, my truancy, that I should be so punished?" (*Too Dear*, p. 22). When his mother dies after an accident he immediately interprets her death as a punishment for his having disobeyed Helena: "Not easy to escape punishment. Was I so important? A thunderstorm and a death. What a petty God, what a miserable-minded God!" (*Too Dear*, p. 67).

The creation of an artistically gifted and sensitive reliable narrator makes it possible to interlace descriptions of events with philosophical comments that add a moral dimension to the novels. Thus in *Too Dear for My Possessing* he can intrude upon the narrative in the character of the grown man and ask: "Was I such a thinking lad? And did I see reasons and motives as clearly as I now pretend? Yet I do not believe I am superimposing my adult mind upon my boy's actions nor that, even if all I have implied is true, I was more sensitive than other children of my age" (p. 68). This device has the effect of cutting away the ground from under the feet of potential critics by anticipating their criticism. Later it also helps to convey the meaning of an incident. For example the meeting with Cecil is endowed with the special quality it had for the teenage boy: "had I not seen more than childishness in her should I have made her the totem-object of my fancy, have made her my familiar, my *doppelgänger*? It is possible that for the first time she awakened sex interest in me. Faugh! And fiddlesticks. I hear the hounds in full cry. What a bother to make about a boy of thirteen, a girl of twelve! And you don't know the meaning of *doppelgänger* but have written it down because it's a nice word. I answer you this; that never would I have made Georges my ghost, or Pieter; and that if Cecil in the flesh were Cecil only, her ghost was my reflection in her image, myself disguised. So you see, I mean what I say" (*Too Dear*, p. 80). Whereas in *Too Dear for My Possessing* the mature man provides a perspective on the young boy, in *An Avenue of Stone* and *A Summer to Decide* other characters frequently comment on Claud and his way of seeing and analyzing things. Thus Charmian can ask Claud "You think you know about people don't you? Well, you don't know about me" (*Avenue*, p. 308). Field can accuse Claud of blaming people too easily (*Summer*, p. 311), and Ellen can advise him, "Don't try too hard to fit everyone into your own pattern, Claud, or something will happen to shake you some day" (*Summer*, p. 329). The comments of all these people are included in Claud's conversations with them so that a corrective to Claud's view of himself is supplied by the opinions of the people around him.

The use that Johnson makes of a narrator in the trilogy gives these novels a moral and philosophical dimension that she tried, with less success, to give *The Monument*. There she failed because the narrator placed in the monument was too abstract and removed. In the trilogy Claud is a fully developed character at the same time as he has acquired an objective view of the events he is reporting. Johnson makes similar use of the device in two of her later novels, *An Impossible Marriage*, and *The Last Resort*.

In the trilogy the author succeeds in combining her interest in inward experience with an objective analysis of it. She is also able to focus on human relationships and integrate a view of the individual with a view of the society in which he lives. These are her main assets as a writer of fiction and together help to explain why the trilogy occupies such a central position in her work.

Chapter Six

Obsessive Passions

Pamela Hansford Johnson's second novel, *Blessed Above Women*, leaves the impression of its being very different from her first one. Nevertheless there are elements in *This Bed Thy Centre* which reveal the author's interest in themes related to the main subject of *Blessed Above Women*. A contemporary reviewer remarks on the fact that "there was a strain of sadism, of conscious brutality, in *This Bed Thy Centre*. It reappears, only much more emphatically, in this curious story of an eccentric and tormented old maid."[1] Although many of Johnson's novels reveal her interest in the perverse side of human behavior and the power of repressed emotion to drive people toward violent action, it becomes the main theme in only three novels: *Blessed Above Women* (1936), *The Trojan Brothers* (1944), and *The Holiday Friend* (1972). All three can be described as studies of a perverse passion that becomes an obsession. In the first, an elderly spinster, Miss Hobchick, develops a fierce love for her young pupil, Joah Sullivan, which eventually drives her mad; in the second, a mature and gifted music-hall comedian is driven to murder the woman who plays games with his feelings for her, and in the third, the indomitable passion of a young art student for her married teacher is obscurely linked with the death of his only child. In each case, the author explores the psychology of the protagonist and conveys the workings of a mind under severe emotional stress with considerable power.

The novel that Pamela Hansford Johnson was engaged in writing at the time of her death reveals the persistence of her interest in the psychology of such people. The novel is based on the true story of the trial of Adelaide Bartlett for the murder of her husband with liquid chloroform in 1886. She was acquitted for lack of evidence. Johnson found the case was full of bizarre details and was interested in presenting the story from the point of view of the woman (interview with the author May 25, 1979).

Blessed Above Women

Cecilia Hobchick, the protagonist of Blessed Above Women, develops an ardent affection for her pupil, Joah, when he is only six years old. Her devotion to the young boy and the reasons behind it are made plain in a "prelude" to the main action of the book which takes place eighteen years later.

In the Prelude, Miss Hobchick, an unattractive spinster of thirty-eight, is shown living with her widowed father and running her own school. She has suffered severely through the loss of her younger, more beautiful sister, Lydia, of whom she was secretly jealous and of whom she makes a saint in her memory. Her father seems to hate her and to take sadistic pleasure in making her feel old and ugly. She is jealous of a younger colleague, Milly Legge, who eventually marries the young man Miss Hobchick fancied for herself. Her sexual frustration is clearly revealed in a strange episode where she is assualted by the village halfwit and then suffers from the delusion that she is pregnant. The doctors advise her father to put her away in the local mental asylum where she spends two dreadful years.

The next chapter opens on Miss Hobchick as the landlady of a boarding house in Bloomsbury. She has two residents, a sadistic masculine woman, Miss Lauderdale, who enjoys bullying people and tormenting animals, and a clever Indian student, Mr. Latta, who writes a successful book and moves away. Joah reenters Miss Hobchick's life as a lodger. He is an aspiring author and comes to London where he has obtained employment. His arrival reawakens Miss Hobchick's long buried desires and she bitterly resents his love for a young dance teacher, Ruth. She finds out that Ruth has been the mistress of Joah's best friend, an artist named Savior, and intends to tell Joah of the affair in order to break his engagement with Ruth. However, Ruth is wise enough to tell Joah herself and, after a brief period of estrangement, the two of them are reconciled. Savior, too deeply in love with Ruth to imagine life without her, commits suicide, and Miss Hobchick, unable to deal with her frustrated love, loses her sanity once more.

The title is taken from the Book of Judges and the relevant lines are quoted in an epigraph. Jael, the wife of Heber, took Sisera, an enemy of the people of Israel, into her tent. She provided him with shelter and food but she killed him while he lay sleeping by driving a nail through his temples, thus freeing the people of Israel from the yoke of the King of Canaan. In the novel, the allusion is made explicit when Miss Hobchick goes to church and listens to a sermon on Jael: "Jael was a great favourite of hers, Jael, the good caterer, the butter-bearer, such an excellent spouse that she did not flinch even from the task of slaying naughty Sisera with her own hands."[2] Miss Hobchick is identified with Jael because she takes Joah into her home, and the importance that she attaches to feeding him well is stressed throughout the novel. At the end of the book, Miss Hobchick suddenly sees Joah as her enemy because he is about to marry Ruth: "In the darkness of her mind she had confounded son with spouse, spouse with son, son and spouse with foe" (p. 309). She gets out of bed, goes and looks at Joah as he lies sleeping and then creeps down into the hallway to find a hammer and a nail. As she stands there searching, she suddenly realizes what she is about to do and stops herself in time.

The parallel between Miss Hobchick and Jael is not extended to Joah and Sisera. Instead, Joah is shown as a young man with a great deal left to learn. His inexperience is contrasted with Ruth's sophistication. He tells Ruth that it gives him a shock to realize that Miss Hobchick and Milly fought over him at school (p. 113), but is blind to the fact that she loves him even more passionately than she did then. He fails to see that Savior is in love with Ruth and finds it very hard to accept Ruth's confession of having lived with Savior. He also does not realize that he has made a lifelong enemy of Miss Lauderdale for having seen her tormenting Miss Hobchick's cat. In fact, he tells Ruth that he is surprised that Miss Lauderdale seems to have forgotten the entire incident. This is far from the truth, however, for Miss Lauderdale has deliberately arranged to let Miss Hobchick find out about Ruth's liaison with Savior as a way of revenging herself upon Joah.

Narrative Technique

In this novel Pamela Hansford Johnson switches between scenes showing Miss Hobchick's restricted life and the life that Joah and his artistic friends lead in London. The scenes dealing with Miss Hobchick present her point of view, but there is also an indication of the way other characters see her. Ruth realizes that she is in love with Joah and, as befits her name, feels genuine pity for the love-starved woman. Savior finds her a pure "period piece" and determines to paint a portrait of her. This portrait proves to be a great success and helps Savior to obtain several commissions. Joah himself is fond of his teacher and was both terrified and adoring when a little boy. The novel he is writing is called "Deadalive," and it reflects Miss Hobchick's situation. When she comes upon this novel in his room and reads it she is very upset by his description of a lonely old maid in love with a young boy. Joah's novel is the only indication in the book that he understands the nature of Miss Hobchick's affection for him.

The intensity of Miss Hobchick's feelings is conveyed by the use of a stream-of-consciousness technique. She lives in a world that constantly borders on the insane. She talks to herself and struggles with devils whom she feels are present in the room when she is alone. She has erected a secret shrine for her dead sister in her bedroom. She is full of passionate hatred when Joah's friends bring him home drunk after celebrating his engagement and many of the things that happen to her haunt her thoughts in a mad way. One such incident can serve as an example. On her way home from shopping, she sees a small boy playing with a ball in the park, he speaks a few words to her, and a moment or so later he is run over by a car. The scene is immediately presented through Miss Hobchick's eyes: "There was the child in the roadway, his legs straddled out, his green suit messy with blood. He had no face at all, but a big red peony in the place of it" (p. 197). Her subsequent thoughts have the confused logic of an extremely agitated mind. She catches sight of a red poster advertising the *Echo* and the slogan "Everyone reads the 'Echo'" imprints itself on her thoughts:

EVERYONE READS THE "ECHO." Fancy fifty people in a tram-car all reading the same thing, each knowing the other's news. To-morrow there will be a dreadful accident in the papers. No, that won't do. Careful, Cecilia, keep calm now and you'll leave the worst time behind you. What did they sell in the shop? There was glass about and something that shone like metal. A woman who tried to take my hat off caught her fingernail in my hair. Things like that accident happen all over the world every day. It might have happened to Joah when he was a baby. Careful, oh, careful, Cecilia! The roses out in the garden at home, in the garden that was mine. The rambler was weak at first; we thought it would rot away but suddenly it bloomed until the whole wall was red with it. The white tree by the sundial must be nearly finished. Mary, Mary, quite contrary, how does your garden grow? That's a pretty nursery rhyme, almost a poem. I wonder if children still love nursery rhymes? The poor little boy will never hear another. (pp. 198–99)

In this passage the way her thoughts jump from the scene of the accident to the shop, to the boy Joah, to her home, and back to the accident makes it easy for the reader to understand her agitation. After this incident a single phrase forms itself in Miss Hobchick's mind and is then used as a kind of refrain: "I shall never again think of a little child without blood on him." The association with death and blood is subsequently reinforced when Miss Hobchick finds a wounded pigeon on her lawn and has to kill it to put it out of its pain. She is shocked to discover that she finds it pleasant to kill (p. 257).

The cumulative effect of these and similar incidents is to prepare the reader for a violent climax with the result that when Miss

Hobchick does not kill Joah the ending seems unsatisfactory. Miss Hobchick driven mad and killing the boy she loves would be a more artistically appropriate ending than Miss Hobchick stopping herself in time and thinking of returning to a lunatic asylum with sudden tranquillity. This failure to resolve the tension created in the book with a fitting climax is probably the reason why some critics feel that in this book the author is reveling "unduly in the unpleasant and the macabre"[3]—the unpleasant incidents become gratuitous instead of necessary.

A consideration of the style in this novel shows it to be full of images and evocative description. For example, the first paragraph describes the village as being bounded on one side by the sea "like a long green animal ready to roar at the stranger who came too suddenly upon its lair," and on the other by "the batwinged tower of the local asylum" (p. 1). Joah is terrified of both. The "batwinged tower" plays an important role in the novel since Miss Hobchick is put away there once for a period of two years and is to return there at the end of the book. The tower is also associated with a "batwinged cloud" that temporarily mars the clear sky that the two lovers Joah and Ruth see on the beautiful summer's day on which they agree to become married. The disturbing association with "the batwinged tower" is borne out by the course of events when Miss Hobchick's obsession threatens to destroy the relationship between Ruth and Joah.

Whereas the use of the "batwinged tower" is thus accommodated within the wider framework of the novel, the sea, which is emphasized a good deal in the first chapter, is not used in a similar manner. In an early episode, Miss Hobchick uses her knowledge of Joah's fear of the sea to punish him for having shown some poems he had written to Milly Legge instead of to her. The scene is a memorable one:

Drawing his socks off, she caressed the small bones of his ankle. She lifted him from the rock. Grasping his arm, she dragged him with her to the green lion that roared for his blood. Bitterly he resisted, his lesser fears lost in this great one. Just as they came to the outer wash of foam along the ribbed sand, he tried to bite her wrist. She slapped him violently and his tears ceased. He stared at her, completely lost.

Then she fell on her knees at his side, rubbing her face upon his own, kissing his eyes, his forehead and his ears.

"Oh, we shan't paddle, shall we my darling, not if we don't like it?"

Closing his eyes, he shook his head.

"No, we won't, we won't. Joah shan't splash in the nasty sea."

Loving her passionately, he dared not speak. Suddenly she said to him, "But why don't we show Miss Hobchick our pieces of poetry? Why do we write them for horrid old Miss Legge?" (pp. 11–12)

This passage contains a repetition of the image of the sea "like a long green animal ready to roar" and the reader is justified in expecting the sea to play a significant part in the development of the novel. In fact, however, the sea is only used as an isolated element and not as a structural unit.

Another example of a potentially significant image which does not live up to its promise is the description of the creeper in Miss Hobchick's garden at home in the long passage quoted earlier: "The rambler was weak at first; we thought it would rot away but suddenly it bloomed until the whole wall was red with it." This description of the rambler draws attention to itself and contains symbolic implications, but it cannot be interpreted as an image of Miss Hobchick's love, or of Joah's situation. Such symbols give the novel an intensity of tone but failure to relate them to the central theme of the novel leaves the reader with a sense of dissatisfaction. It is as if the writer were using images and descriptions for their own sake rather than subordinating them to a controlling design. This weakness is probably the reason why, although a sinister atmosphere is effectively created, the novel lacks the artistic sophistication that a well worked out use of symbols could have given to it.

Pamela Hansford Johnson's next assay into this type of fiction, *The Trojan Brothers*, is a greater achievement precisely because she is more discriminating in her use of certain images, and their recurrent use is justified by their place in the central design.

The Trojan Brothers

The Trojan Brothers also deals with the theme of obsessive passion. In this novel the victim of his own tormented feelings is Sidney Nichols, a widower of thirty-six, who falls in love with his snobbish cousin, a married society lady named Betty Todd. The novel is neatly structured and carefully balanced. It is, in the words of Jane Martin, "the most tightly knit and satisfying narrative she has yet produced."[4] The story is told in three parts of equal length. The first shows the way in which Sid's growing love for Betty destroys his relationship with his mother and his two closest friends. Part Two shows Sid left on his own after the sudden death of his mother and his quarrel with his friends Benny and Maggie. He is totally absorbed in his clandestine affair with Betty who refuses to divorce her husband because of the status she enjoys as his wife. The second part ends with the abrupt termination of Sid's relationship with Betty because she has found a new lover. Part Three shows Sidney's return to his friends, his vain effort to grapple with heartbreak, his mounting jealousy of Betty's new lover, and his rage against Betty which culminates in his murdering her. An Epilogue places the main action in the past and relates the story to the contemporary scene in London.

Critical Analysis

Sidney and his cousin are contrasted with each other. Betty's mother, Sidney's aunt, marries above her and forgets all about her poor relations. Betty herself moves in a world completely outside Sidney's grasp. She is a social climber, who wants to gain a reputation as a great party-giver, and who does not hesitate to use people for her own ends. Every scene that describes Betty shows her at a party, at a ball, at the theater, as a society hostess. Her glittering glamorous world is shallow and false, her friends spiteful and hypocritical. Sidney, on the other hand, is a philosophic man. He lives with his widowed mother, is proud of belonging to the working class, works hard at his profession, and has two very sincere friends,

Benny and Maggie, who care for his well-being. He is generous and charitable, taking a poor girl, Anna, under his wing, and seeing that she finds work with his team. Anna herself develops a strong and abiding love for Sid which is a parallel to his love for Betty and a contrast to Betty's way of dealing with Sid.

When Sid first meets Betty he is determined to humiliate her in return for the way she humiliated his grandmother. Even when she allows him to become her lover, he is conscious of the fact that she despises him for his lower-class origins. His entire relationship with Betty is shown in terms of a compulsive fascination which will inevitably lead to disaster.

According to Jane Martin, Sidney "is believable only so long as he sticks to his normal role: a squat freckled man with a clown's face and a philosopher's mind. When he gives way to his obsessive love for cousin Betty Todd, who marries out of her class, his behavior needs more explaining than is to be read into Miss Johnson's rather misty analysis. Quiet Englishmen of lower middle age and class, who from birth have been inhaling the class system with their daily fresh air, are not apt to contract dark, sadistic obsessions from a cousinly snob."[5] This judgment does not give enough credit to the skill with which Johnson foreshadows the climax from the very beginning of the novel. She succeeds in making the picture of Sid's obsession convincing by showing how easily Sid is excited and angered. As soon as he sees Betty in the audience in the theater where he is playing his part as the hind-legs of a comic horse, he recalls an ancient grudge. He has never forgotten how Betty spurned his grandmother on the only visit she paid the old lady before she died —his grandmother went forward to kiss Betty and she turned a "cheek like cast-iron" to her in a way that made Sid feel that he could have murdered her.[6] When Betty and her husband come backstage to demand an apology, Sid is adamant in his refusal and is described as being "elated with rage." The comments he makes as soon as they leave—"She wasn't worth to have shined up my old Gran's shoes with her own spit" and "Dazzler, isn't she?" (p. 15)— immediately reveal his ambivalent attitude towards Betty, a mixture of vengeful dislike and irresistible attraction.

Even in his dealings with his best friends, Benny and his wife Maggie, Sid is shown as a person capable of taking delight in hurting the people he loves. For example, when Maggie will not agree to perform at a party that Betty is planning to give, Sid says: "I can manage all right without you Maggie. Even as he spoke, he felt his heart lift in the delight of doing something stupid and cruel. He noted his mother's gesture of distress and was excited by it" (p. 53).

In addition to showing Sid's excitable nature the author develops several extremely effective devices for making the picture of Sid's mental state convincing. One is the recurrent use of the image of a wooden doll as a symbol for Betty. The first time he sees her in the theater he thinks of her as "a woman painted like a pierrot doll" (p. 7). Later the same image recurs in one of Sid's dreams:

Subtly, and at first without his realization, the new nightmare began to hatch, the noise of it rustling in his head like a fowl in straw. He took Betty Todd down the lurid corridors of the night, his hands clapped to her cheeks that she might not peel off her mask. Her powder was between his fingers like the rheumatic's chalk, stiffening and chilling them. After a while they stopped, and he drew off her dress. Beneath it she was naked, but her nakedness was wooden, and she was jointed like a doll with inches of string. He began to jeer at her because she was so thin, to jeer at her and to take her, jeering at her because her body was ugly and taking her because she was a lady and would hate his hands. (p. 27)

The same image is recalled in Sid's thoughts of Betty before her party:

Then his thoughts strayed . . . bearing him through blinded alleys to a white room that knew darkness in its own terms, a room where she dangled like a pierrot doll between floor and ceiling, the sawdust hot as blood in her slack body. As he approached her she blew out on wires towards him, her lids fluttering with love, her mouth many-petalled as a carnation, her whole body melting to a yes, and yes again. He thought, I am no lower than you, no less fit than any other man to take you. You and Lucy spoke the same language, you could have been at ease with each other; and I wasn't too low for her. Your swank's like an onion, peel it away and away and there's nothing left. I shall take you when I please. (pp. 56–57)

The thoughts in this passage echo not only the image of the pierrot doll but also reveal the injured pride of a man who feels rejected because of his class and foreshadow a violent end.

The connection between Betty and Sid's first wife, Lucy, is one that also sets up a series of echoes. Sid feels guilty because Lucy married him against her father's wishes and died in childbirth soon afterwards. He feels responsible for her death and accuses himself of having murdered her. It is clearly stated that since his wife's death "he had never wished to marry nor to form an intimacy outside of marriage, because he feared, in some cell of his mind too deep to take the light of conscious expression, that he might kill another woman. He had slain. He would slay again. Because, in the code of his own law, love must lead to permanency, he had safeguarded himself from the danger of falling in love, knowing that if he should settle his desire upon a girl he would then want to have her by him by day and by night, enclosing her in the fences of his own prodigious fidelity" (p. 72). When he does fall in love with Betty, who is the epitome of infidelity, it is plausible that Sid's possessive love will lead to disaster. The fact that he feels he has "killed" his first wife (albeit metaphorically) foreshadows the murder of Betty.

Another device that helps to make Sidney's obsession convincing is the frequent recounting of his nightmarish dreams and fancies in regard to Betty. Even when he is at the height of his love for her he translates his desire into daydreams that are full of "sadistic imagery":

The pictures began with one of a long bare road of high houses, their plaster peeled and yellowish in the glare of the moon. Stepping out from a side street she walked swiftly away, her back turned to him. After a while she began to run, now and then looking back over her shoulder, her face furtive with fear. He pursued her, slowly at first, then doggedly gaining: and then was the horror he could not endure.

He fought this first picture as a boy fights the first insidious image of his private fantasy. (p. 73)

This daydream is a prophetic image of the way in which he chases Betty in the final scene, and the reader is reminded of it just before Betty breaks off her relationship with Sid. The two of them are walking across the fields near Betty's country home toward a public house when Sid's nightmare vision returns to him:

He saw one of the little pictures that had frightened him long ago. There was a long blank road of high houses down which she walked, her feet scarcely seeming to touch the ground. He knew she was afraid of something, for once or twice she twisted her head over her shoulder, exposing a face livid and blank in the light of an invisible moon. From a side turning a man, stocky, his domed head bare, silently emerged and went trotting in her wake, keeping so precisely behind her that even when she looked round she could not catch a glimpse of him. He was gaining on her, gaining a yard with every step; and then as if she sensed pursuit, she began to run, to run, to run, not towards shelter but to a great fire that had sprung up like a devil in her path. (p. 171)

The image of the fire at the end of this vision reminds Sid that he suspects Betty of having deliberately let her husband die in a fire because he had surprised her by announcing his intention of divorcing her. Now as he walks with her, some devil prompts him to accuse Betty, who seizes the opportunity to break off their relationship since she has become interested in a famous author, Arnold Dench.

As soon as they enter the pub towards which they were walking Betty is described as a "dutch doll of a woman" (p. 171). The previous images of a doll dangling from the ceiling and of a woman running from a man in fear combine to prepare for the climactic final chase when Sid, driven past bearing, finds his way to Betty's house, locks up her maid, sends away Anna, grimly pursues Betty, and strangles her.

It is a difficult task for the author to describe the actual murder scene, which is both ridiculous and grim, without degenerating into melodrama. One weakness in the organization of the scene is the introduction of Anna as a participant. Anna's presence is probably meant to heighten the contrast between the two women and to show how Sid fell tragically in love with the wrong one. However, it is difficult to believe that, in spite of her promise to do anything "good or bad" for Sid's sake, Anna would first follow her instinct to go to Betty in order to save Sid from doing anything that might hurt him, and then suddenly be so overcome by weariness as to accept his explanation that he is only going to frighten Betty and agree to go home to sleep. Anna's presence dissipates the effect previously achieved by the accumulation of Sid's nightmare-visions and obsessed thoughts. The reader is suddenly aware of a normal world outside Sid's thoughts and feelings. Several reviewers complain of a sense of inadequacy in the novel and attribute it to Pamela Hansford Johnson's handling of the combination of comedy and tragedy.[7] However, it is not the combination of the comic with the tragic that is responsible for this sense of inadequacy so much as the introduction of another point of view at the crucial moment. Sid's obsessive state has been carefully plotted and if the final scene had been presented exclusively from his point of view, the novel as a whole would have carried greater conviction.

The "Epilogue" adds an unexpected dimension to the story. It explains that the action of the novel took place in the 1920s, and is being told in the 1940s to an audience of enthralled stage hands by an old comedian, Mr. Hockaby, who played a minor part in it. The few brief appearances that Hockaby makes in the tale itself give no indication of his role as the narrator. He is referred to in the third person and is a mildly homosexual actor who lives on the fringes of Betty's social circle. He had been exploited by her in the past and tries to warn Sid against her.

Apart from serving as a way of letting the reader know that Sid was hanged, the only reason for introducing him as the narrator in an epilogue seems to be the possibility of placing Sidney's personal tragedy against a wider perspective. When Mr. Hockaby tells the story, the Second World War has broken out, and he tells it as a means of whiling away the hours they spend as fire-wardens. One of the stage hands comments on the 1920s being "a bit barmy," thus giving Hockaby the opportunity of replying:

"You think so? Because of one murder, and that a useful one? We are enjoying the privilege—I say the privilege—of sitting above London, the most wonderful and secret city in the world, doing our somewhat pathetic "bit" "—he snipped off the word jocosely, fastidiously—"to defend her. Down there, this autumn, this winter, there have been hundred upon hundred of entirely useless murders, officially committed, and quite peculiarly senseless because not one of the murderers has been injured by his victim." (pp. 233–34)

The stage hand, who is a budding Socialist, tries to justify the need to fight Hitler but the conversation soon peters out.

In her novels Pamela Hansford Johnson often makes the effort to link the affairs of individual people with the problems of the world at large, but in *The Trojan Brothers* the connection is too abruptly introduced in a brief Epilogue. Although it is true that Sidney is painfully aware of class-distinctions and resents the fact that Betty feels she is his superior, in the main story these feelings act as a way of showing the measure of Sid's frustration in his relationship with Betty. In spite of the laudability of the aim of trying to include a historical perspective in this novel it remains extraneous to the essential theme. The author, in this novel, is at her best when she concentrates upon the psychology of frustrated emotion, and shows how a person can be driven to extremes by the force of an overwhelming passion.

The Holiday Friend

The Holiday Friend, Johnson's third variation on the theme of obsessive passion, is a more complex book than either *Blessed Above Women* or *The Trojan Brothers.* The "holiday friend" of the title at first describes Melissa Hirst, a young art student who decides to pursue her art-history teacher, Gavin Eastwood, to the Belgian seaside resort where he usually spends his vacations with his wife and son. She arrives there, plans an "accidental meeting," and pushes her friendship upon the happily married couple.

The fortnight that they spend together is taken up with all the usual pastimes of people on holiday by the sea. The setting of the cozy resort, Les Roseaux, with its friendly café and hotel owners is admirably created. There are visits to the beach, to "the golf," walks along the promenade, and the occasional highlight—a mechanical band, a circus, or a fair. This surface of relaxed holiday life is distubed by an undercurrent of tension and menace. The tension is created partly by Melissa's obsession, for she is so driven by her passion for Gavin that she seizes hold of every opportunity to be with him and evoke a response. Then it is augmented by the strange behavior of the Eastwood's overprotected eleven-year-old son, Giles, a sensitive boy who contracts a secret friendship with a mysterious Flemish youth. Finally, the weather, which is frequently stormy and rainy, also heightens the sinister atmosphere.

In terms of plot nothing much seems to happen except for the meetings between Melissa and the Eastwoods and their realization that she is in love with Gavin. The Eastwoods feel they have the situation under control when, suddenly, on the last day of their holiday their peace is completely shattered by the disappearance of their son. Panic-stricken, they set out to look for him and meet Melissa, who joins them in their desperate search. Melissa is the one to find the body. Tied tight around his neck is the tie with a pattern of green snakes on it that his Flemish friend was described as wearing, and on the sand beside him lie the jacks that he used to play with this nameless friend when they met in secret by the sand dunes. Melissa longs to comfort Gavin in his grief, but he looks at her with such hatred that she realizes that any hope she may have cherished of gaining his love is lost forever.

There are a few minor characters who surround the inner circle composed of Gavin Eastwood, his wife, Hannah, their son, Giles, and Gavin's unwanted admirer, Melissa. Another family, John and Vera Venning and their daughter Chloe, forms a contrast to the Eastwoods because the husband and wife are always quarreling.

There is a German family, the Fischers, whose son Hans is an unwanted companion for Giles. There is an American, Jean, who admires Melissa and pursues her in a way that acts as a parallel to
her own admiration of Gavin, and there is Bob Conrad, who develops an innocent admiration for Hannah that both contrasts with
and recalls Melissa's admiration for Gavin. He also acts as an observer of the "human drama" that unfolds. As is evident from this
summary presentation of the characters, there is more than one
"holiday friend" in the story. In fact most of the holiday friendships
acquired during this fortnight seem to be unwelcome. One of
Gavin's casual remarks is especially pertinent: "These holiday
friendships . . . sometimes have very little to commend them."[8]
He is referring to the fact that his son, Giles, does not want to play
with Hans, but the remark can be extended to apply to the way he
feels about Melissa, and the way Melissa feels about Jean. Ironically
enough, the only friends who are wanted are Giles's mysterious
friend, who is probably responsible for his death, and Gavin by
Melissa. A parallel between Giles and Melissa suggests itself here
because Gavin's friendship brings her nothing but desolation (p.
253).

Narrative Technique

The book is constructed so that chapters giving the point of view
of the Eastwoods and of Melissa alternate with each other. A few
chapters also give the point of view of Giles, who feels that his
parents fuss over him too much and who longs to be left alone to
meet the friend who has imposed secrecy upon him in some un-
spoken way. Occasionally the author presents the same event from
two different points of view. Thus the initial meeting between
Melissa and Gavin on the beach is presented first as Gavin experienced it—as a chance meeting with a casual acquaintance—and then
as Melissa arranged it—with great care to create the right effect of
coincidence. At times the author deliberately breaks the chronological sequence of events in order to increase the tension. For example,
when telling of Giles's final disappearance the author first describes

how Melissa met Gavin and Hannah on the promenade, "their faces white," and then moves back in time to show how the events of that day led up to this dramatic moment.

In this book Pamela Hansford Johnson makes effective use of a device that she has used in previous novels, but in a less noticeable fashion. She introduces the words of songs and music as a way of revealing inward experience. In *Blessed Above Women* songs tend to fasten in Miss Hobchick's mind. Albert in *The Monument* also has stanzas of songs echoing in his brain, and in *Too Dear for My Possessing* Claud's memory of Cecil is associated with her theme song, but in *The Holiday Friend* the same tendency becomes much more pronounced. Both Melissa and Gavin are aware of the songs they hear, and their power to recall certain people and occasions is specifically mentioned. Gavin, lying in bed after an eventful day, hears music arising from the terrace: "A classical record this time, after all the pop; he thought he recognised it. Yes he did, Satie's *Gymnopédies*. He had had an old 78 of it once. He knew he would always associate it with this day, with Giles, with Hannah, with Melissa, and he damned the capacity of music to make itself into a theme-song. Memory was strong enough without its persistent interference" (p. 168). After this, whenever he sings or hums this tune in the book it has a special significance. In the same way Melissa hears "J'attendrai" and the author comments: "She would never, for the rest of her life, hear it without thinking of him" (p. 226).

Both these quotations also serve to show how Johnson has adopted third-person narration even when she reveals the thoughts of her characters instead of the stream-of-consciousness flow of thoughts that she used so noticeably in her early novels *This Bed Thy Centre*, and *Blessed Above Women*. In her later novels the passages where she tries to mirror the actual flow of thoughts are few and far between. In *The Holiday Friend* Melissa's state is not only revealed by reporting her feelings, it is also commented on by other characters. Bob Conrad, for example, tells a colleague of Gavin's that she has "got some sort of fixation about Mr. Eastwood" and that "she follows him around and seems to be disturbed in her mind" (p. 188–89). Hannah and Gavin think of it as "Melissa's obsession" and Gavin wonders "if she were a little mad" (p. 200).

Whereas Johnson has discarded the stream-of-consciousness technique she still includes the dreams and fantasies of her characters to show the intensity of their emotional state. Like Miss Hobchick and Sid, Melissa indulges in fantasies: "She lay under the leaves and giving herself up to her imaginings. This time she went further than the embrace and the impassioned kiss; they were together, naked, in the high bright room and he was making love to her, gently at first, and then to the piercing climax. She was carried away by this to the point of shock, almost shocked to her senses" (p. 87). These fantasies reveal the intensity of her desire. She also has recurrent dreams which can be interpreted in Freudian terms. In particular she dreams about a fairground stunt she has seen where Captain Keppel climbed to the top of a high mast to perform acrobatic feats. This mast becomes a symbol of her frustrated sexuality:

Melissa dreamed that she was climbing a great crimson mast, up into the sky. She could see above her an octagonal lantern, like that of a lighthouse; her feet were bare on the glittering rigging. She was climbing and yet she sat in the square below watching herself. It was perilous; she was afraid all the time that she might fall, but she knew she must go on. To reach the lantern, to grip it, to crawl inside it, where joy awaited her; she must do this. Her feet were bleeding; she saw her other self, quiet on the benches, watch the slow black drops splash on the cobbles. Her body ached; all her bones were strained to the ascent. (p. 129)

This dream of Melissa's foreshadows a violent ending in the same way that Sid's dream of Betty did. At the top of the mast she finds she cannot get to her goal: "Her hands, slipping in rain or blood gave way; she fell, but slowly, cushioned in air, wrapped in its comfort" (p. 129). There is violence at the end of The Holiday Friend but somewhat unexpectedly it is Gavin's son, Giles, and not Melissa, who is killed.

Theme

A few of the critics who reviewed this book felt that there was a discrepancy between the story of Melissa's unrequited love and the death of the little boy. In the *New Yorker*, for example, the reviewer complains about "a number of bewildering mysterious figures who pop up and disappear like fireflies. What are they up to? What, if anything, do they have to do with the book's gruesome ending? One asks in vain."[9] The critic in the *Times Literary Supplement* expresses a similar sense of bewilderment: "It is never clear how ugly the author intends her petite plage to seem." He finds that the novel "leaves one impatient, uneasy, with a sense of claustrophobia."[10] It is therefore worthwhile to try to elucidate the meaning of Giles's death.

First of all it is evident that Giles's disappearance is well prepared for by the use of foreshadowing. On the first day they spend at the beach Gavin cannot find Giles: "His heart misgave him. But what harm could he get to, among these people? He began to call. There was no reply, but he found him at last in a hollow, lying on his face, scraping up the dry powder and letting it trickle between his fingers" (p. 23). On another occasion Giles is playing in the sand and covers himself up to the neck with it. Melissa's comment that he looks frightening "just a head lying by itself" is emphasized by the fact that Giles then finds it difficult to get out of the sand he has buried himself in (p. 45). When Giles is left in Melissa's care she falls asleep dreaming of his father and wakes up to find that he has disappeared. After an agonized search she finds him playing by the sand dunes. The fascination that the sand dunes hold for him is also stressed and he frequently demonstrates his wish to be left alone and make his own way there. In a brief chapter placed exactly in the middle of the book, Giles is shown playing jacks with his friend—a blond youth who has a tie with a pattern of green snakes on it. He meets the same boy again at the fairground and confirms an appointment with him. Thus, Giles's frequent disappearances, the fact that he is extremely secretive about meeting his friend, and his fascination with the sand dunes are all stressed in a way that leads up naturally to his final disappearance.

It is more difficult to explain why he has to die and how his death is related to the theme of Melissa's obsessive love for Gavin. Johnson has provided a clue that is worth pursuing. Twice in the novel Gavin's wife, Hannah, thinks of Ibsen's play *Little Eyolf* in relation to her son: "There was nothing either liked so much as the company of the other; even Giles, whom they loved so much, interrupted that. Hannah was reminded of *Little Eyolf*, of Allmers's dreams of gold and green forests, and her comfort momentarily fled; for the sake of their passion, Rita and her husband had let the little boy be lamed for life. We are not like that to Giles, though, he comes first" (p. 217). The second reference to *Little Eyolf* comes toward the end of the same chapter when Hannah and Gavin sit out in the "serene" night and feel desire rising within them. Hannah thinks once more of her child: "Little Eyolf unharmed. She wondered how she had let this thought, with its token threat, intrude. She was not Rita, nor Gavin Allmers; Giles was wrapped around in their care, too much so, maybe, but safely" (p. 221). The fact that her sense of security is false and that Giles is not safe is proved brutally not long afterwards, when, on the last day of their holiday, he is strangled while his parents sit in the hotel lounge reminiscing about their honeymoon (p. 248).

The allusion to *Little Eyolf* is explicit enough to merit further analysis. Allmers, in Ibsen's play, is a writer who is working on a book to be called "Human Responsibility." There are two women in his life, his wife, Rita, a dark and passionate woman, and his supposed half-sister, Asta, a blond and virtuous lady. The one stands for physical and the other for spiritual love. Allmers betrays both these women. He also has a son, Little Eyolf, whom he betrays. His egoistical dream is to see his son finish the book that he himself has given up hope of writing. His son, Eyolf, is lame both physically and spiritually. When the Rat-wife comes to Allmers's house asking him if he has any rats that need to be drowned, Eyolf is fascinated by her and accompanies her to the waterside where he drowns. The imagery of green and gold, and the association of water with death run right through Ibsen's play.

There are many parallels between *The Holiday Friend* and *Little Eyolf*. Gavin is a teacher of art history who tells Melissa, toward the end of their holiday, that he is going to write a book. He too is caught between two women, his wife, with whom he has an erotic and passionate relationship, and Melissa, with whom his friendship is on a more spiritual plane: "No fantasy of touching her could enter his mind" (p. 221), yet "he knew he had in some innocent measure responded to her feeling" (p. 161). In a sense he betrays them both. Inevitably, Gavin's friendship with Melissa leads him to conceal things from his wife for the first time in their marriage. At the same time he feels the only way he can escape from Melissa is by telling his wife of her love for him: "He knew it meant throwing Melissa to the lions, but he needed Hannah's help" (p. 164). Once he has told his wife, he knows "that to Melissa this conversation, so light in tone if not in feeling, would have seemed an ultimate betrayal" (p. 167). In the end he puts Melissa off quite cruelly and destroys all hope in her: "Blind with shock, she ran off from the dunes, through the long desolation, the future that held nothing for her" (p. 253).

Although the parents are overanxious and protective about their son it is frequently mentioned that they "sometimes had a selfish longing to be alone together, just the two of them, but they had always brushed this aside as unworthy" (p. 19). An incident concerning Giles's school report shows that they do not understand him. When they see his anxiety just before opening his report they decide to burn it, unread. They are puzzled when Giles rushes out crying and Gavin has an uneasy feeling that he has done the wrong thing (pp. 25–28). Later a letter from the headmaster tells them that it was an unusually good report (p. 81). The entire episode is symptomatic of their relationship with their son. There is also a slight suggestion of sterility in their marriage because in spite of both of them wanting more children Giles is their only son.

Giles's fascination for the mysterious stranger is akin to Eyolf's fascination for the Rat-wife, and the death that both of them meet through a mysterious stranger is associated with the sea. Even the imagery of green and gold runs through *The Holiday Friend*. The horse that the Flemish youth rides at the fair is a green and gold horse, his blond hair gleams gold, and his tie has a pattern of green snakes upon it.

If, as the above analysis suggests, Pamela Hansford Johnson is making deliberate use of *Little Eyolf* as a frame of reference for *The Holiday Friend*, then it is worth considering the possibility of the novel's having a similar or related theme. This play, even more than Ibsen's other works, deals with the question of human responsibility and the betrayal of love. Is it too farfetched to suggest that, in a very different form, Johnson is exploring the same theme? Without a doubt Melissa is obsessed by her love for Gavin and it gives her no peace. However, she tries to stop herself from loving him. She even prays, "Oh, God, if you are anywhere at all, listen; make me not love him. For I cannot bear it" (p. 172).

There is a moment in the book when Hannah is critical of Gavin for describing Melissa as "a bit of a bore" to a colleague of his. She feels a strong wave of pity for Melissa: "She determined that she would try to be kind. If this girl was in love with Gavin, so much the worse for her. Before Hannah had met him, she had had a young, greenstick passion which had been denied; she could not forget that, the awful heat, the awful chill. She looked at her husband in a moment's disenchantment, but a moment was all it was" (p. 78). Hannah and Melissa are also identified with each other in the scene when they both ride on the merry-go-round at the fair. Hannah calls out that she feels like Joan of Arc and Giles tells her that "Melissa felt like that" as well (p. 212). Yet in spite of her feeling for Melissa and her realization that Melissa needs compassion she is aware of being cruel to her: "But I have been a little cruel" (p. 103), she says, and again: "I wish I didn't have a sneaking feeling that it would be cruelty. Why should I care about being cruel to her?" (p. 182). Gavin is also aware that he should show Melissa pity: "It seemed to him that they had enough felicity to spare a little compassion, even a little encouragement, for the

Melissas of this world" (p. 128). Ultimately, however, the married couple, secure in their felicity, present a united front against Melissa, and fail to fulfill their responsibility toward her as a fellow human being. Thus there is a definite relationship between Ibsen's theme in *Little Eyolf* and the theme of *The Holiday Friend*. Taking the resemblance into consideration makes the connection between Giles's death and Melissa's passion less bewildering. Just as Giles's friend betrayed him and killed him physically, Gavin betrays Melissa and kills her spiritually. Gavin and Hannah fail toward both young people.

Although all three of the novels discussed in this chapter provide a thorough exploration of the mind of a person obsessed with a strong, unrequited passion, *The Holiday Friend* goes beyond the previous two books in scope. It deals not only with the psychology of the obsessed but also with the moral problem of the human responsibility and the cruelty involved in depriving the weak and vulnerable of all hope.

Chapter Seven

Love and Marriage

Pamela Hansford Johnson's first novel ended with a picture of a young couple on their wedding night. *The Philistines* (1949) begins with the morning after and tells the story of how two people who begin marriage passionately in love awake to the realities of living together once all passion is spent. The situation of a young woman who marries in haste and repents at leisure is one that Pamela Hansford Johnson develops at some length in the last two books of the Helena trilogy when Claud's half-sister, Charmian, finds that the man she has fallen in love with and married within six weeks is a weak ne'er-do-well. In spite of her mother and half-brother's efforts to persuade her to leave him, Charmian insists on remaining true to the ideal of a good wife who supports her husband through life.

In the three novels that follow *An Avenue of Stone* and *A Summer to Decide* Johnson focuses on the lives of three intelligent and passionate women who make the same mistake as Charmian but who are determined to escape the trap in which they find themselves. Like Nora in Ibsen's *A Doll's House* these women feel hampered and enclosed by the marriages they have made and are strong enough to fight for freedom. Thus Gwen in *The Philistines* (1949) asks for her freedom and gets it unexpectedly when her husband dies in an accident, and the heroines of both *Catherine Carter* (1952) and *An Impossible Marriage* (1954) succeed in obtaining a divorce and marry, more successfully, a second time.

In these three novels and the two that are discussed in the next chapter—novels which A. S. Byatt has fittingly described as "the patient serious novels of the Fifties"—Pamela Hansford Johnson's particular gifts as a novelist are fully displayed.[1] These novels are memorable not only because of the sensitivity of her analysis of intimate human relationships but also because of her ability to create fully rounded characters. In *Important to Me* she says that this is what Proust taught her:

I often wonder what Proust taught me. Nothing, I believe, in surface style and presentation. But he did teach me how to look at, and round, characters. He taught me the trick of false presentation—no one was as he seemed—but I had already learned some of that from Dostoevsky. No, what I learned from him was to study—or try to study (I don't wish to be presumptuous) character in the round. I no longer looked at my people as if they were paintings, two-dimensional. I tried to regard them more in the light of sculptures, with a door at either end of the gallery. According to the door at which one presented one-self, each piece of sculpture would seem different: it was the reconciling of these different aspects that was all-important. (p. 203)

The fact that she learned Proust's lesson well is amply demonstrated by the strength of her characterization in these five novels, where her interest in human relationships and character is at its height. Walter Allen suggests that this is her special contribution to the genre: "It became slowly apparent that, very quietly, Miss Hansford Johnson was extending the territory of the novel. It was not that the types she was describing, or their milieu, were exactly new; but she had made them new. . . . She had seen all round them and caught them in a new light, in a new significance, so that in the end they were somehow bigger, richer as emblems of the human condition than one might have expected them to be."[2] No doubt what Walter Allen describes as "seeing all round" her characters is what Johnson means when she speaks of trying to look at her characters as if they were sculptures.

The reason why character becomes all-important in the group of novels to be discussed in this chapter is because of Johnson's concentration in all three on the theme of marriage. With delicate skill she anatomizes the process whereby two people who are instantly attracted to each other marry, only to find they cannot make a success of marriage. The emphasis in these novels is on the theme of an "impossible marriage," but, especially in *Catherine Carter*, she also explores the makings of a marriage that is likely to endure.

The Philistines

The central character in *The Philistines* is Gwen Hesketh, a gifted young woman who dreams of becoming a writer or a painter. Having lost her father at the age of ten, she has grown up in Clapham living with a dominating mother, who persuades her to study for a degree in sociology and has high ambitions for her daughter. When Gwen, after a disappointment in love, meets Clifford Burgand at a local dance she falls passionately in love with him and does not heed her mother's grim warning: "He is not in our class . . . he doesn't think as you do. He won't like the things you do. You'll just become an ordinary suburban housewife."[3] As things turn out, Gwen's mother's words prove too true. After their marriage Gwen and Clifford live with his widowed mother and maiden sister and the inevitable problems of living with in-laws arise. At first Gwen is anxious to set up house on her own, but the shock of a miscarriage followed soon afterwards by the loss of her mother leaves her in a state of apathy and she resigns herself to the prospect of continuing to live with her husband's family. Her daily life is excessively confined: "She shared in the cooking, did most of the shopping, and in the afternoons amused herself like other Branley women, going to the cinema, playing tennis, chatting in the teashops. She still read a good deal, and was warned every evening by Mrs. Burgand that her eyes would drop out. Sometimes friends came in to play cards. There were occasional dances at the club. There was an almost total absence of any kind of excitement" (p. 20). Gradually, Gwen begins to react against the tedium of her existence. She becomes restless, and disagreements begin to arise among her, her husband, and her in-laws. The birth of a son, Philip, does not do much to help matters as she disagrees with her mother-in-law's ideas about his upbringing. When the Second World War breaks out Clifford enlists, and Gwen takes advantage of the excuse his absence affords her and finds herself a job as almoner at the local hospital. Through her work she meets, and slowly falls in love with, Paul Smith, a doctor who offers her the intellectual stimulation she lacks. When her husband returns from the war he accepts Paul as a friend, but Gwen is torn between the intensity of her longing for Paul and her sense of guilt. The novel moves contrapuntally between scenes showing Paul's life and Gwen's. In time, Gwen confesses her love to Paul but learns he is still in love with a woman who has jilted him and married his beloved elder brother. Unable to find fulfillment with Paul, Gwen continues to chafe against the bonds of her marriage and begs Clifford for a divorce. He refuses to take her seriously and agrees instead to apply for a transfer to another town where they can start afresh. Gwen is dismayed when he brings her news of their transfer to Norfolk, which she envisages as being as provincial as Bradley, but she is too worn out emotionally to do anything. Circumstances work toward her release, however, for Clifford, drunk after an evening out in London, falls out of the train on their return journey and dies as a result of his injuries. After a long and trying period facing the inquest, her neighbors, and her husband's relations, Gwen leaves for London and starts to make a new life for herself.

This novel has received remarkably little notice. In a brief review in the *Times Literary Supplement* the critic feels it "fails primarily because Miss Johnson never convinces us that Gwen is sufficiently imaginative or sensitive to be a misfit in Philistia."[4] It is perhaps unfortunate that the title of the book draws attention to the society in which Gwen finds herself, and can therefore be interpreted as an endorsement of her view of Branley. In fact, the novelist has taken pains to establish an ironic distance to her protagonist—a sculpture should be studied from different points of view. An early example of a double perspective on Gwen is in the description of her grief when she loses her mother. At first it is quite genuine and makes her extremely malleable. After a while, however, she realizes "that the reality of her complaisance has changed into a *performance*, and that she was having to remember to sustain it" (p. 19). This shows both Gwen's desire to play a part and her ability to analyze her own motives. An example of the way the author suggests that Gwen can be wrong is the account of Gwen's reaction towards her friend's suffering. Pamela Mayhew, an unattractive young woman who lives with her widowed mother, is deeply hurt when her fiancé falls in love with, and marries, a flirtatious newcomer to Branley. When Gwen is going through the worst agony of her unrequited love for Paul she thinks of writing a letter to Pamela to tell her how well she understands what she must be suffering. However, she changes her mind, thinking "Pamela has not the intensity of feeling that I have. She could not know this rending" (p. 168). The author comments: "In her arrogance, which was an arrogance born out of the humiliation she could not even now admit, Gwen did not believe that any woman living had suffered so deeply as herself" (p. 168). Events prove that Gwen has underestimated Pamela's capacity for intense feeling. Pamela commits suicide, and when Clifford brings Gwen the tragic news she realizes how wrong her judgment has been (p. 209).

Even in her treatment of Gwen's behavior toward society in Branley the author makes it clear that Gwen is often at fault. She does not try to conceal her poor opinion of her neighbors and they resent the fact that she thinks of herself as intellectually their superior. One of Gwen's neighbors, Mrs. Hedley, tries to give Gwen a word of friendly advice: "Do you realise that you're always snubbing us, or doing something to hurt people's feelings?" (p. 193). Even though Mrs. Hedley is an inveterate gossip who does not invite sympathy, the reader recognizes an element of truth in her words. There are several other instances of a criticism of Gwen. Her behavior as a mother leaves much to be desired. She does not hesitate to break her promise to her son and send him away to a boarding school when it suits her own purpose to be left alone to concentrate upon her emotional problems. The boy clearly suffers on account of this and begins to steal. Later when she is left a widow and has lost all hope of gaining Paul she decides to devote herself to the role of mother. The writer speaks ironically of it taking some time for "the first fever of Gwen's desire for self-immola-tion" to flag (p. 301).

Gwen also sees herself in the light of a champion of the working class and befriends her mother-in-law's charwoman, Mrs. Garnett, when she is falsely accused of having stolen the money that Gwen knows her son has taken. Toward the end of the book Mrs. Garnett returns her kindness but Gwen realizes "with shame, that she was a little tired of Mrs. Garnett. It has seemed so beautiful, this idea of the two of them outcast, helping each other" (p. 302). The effect of these comments is to establish an ironic distance which makes it possible to see Gwen differently from the way she sees herself and to realize that she has a great deal left to learn. The heroine of this book, like Jane Austen's *Emma*, is lacking in self-knowledge. She is full of romantic ideas about herself and intellec-tual arrogance. She has to undergo the painful process of acquiring self-knowledge. At the end of the book she discards her romantic view of herself and recognizes her need to live a full life for her own sake: "I don't want to help others to life—I want to have it myself" (p. 302). The last view the reader has of her is of a young woman on the threshold of a new and fuller life: "sharp to the world as if she were in love" (p. 304).

Style

In this novel Pamela Hansford Johnson is fully in control of her medium. She has developed a style that is unobtrusive yet rich in overtones. There is a remarkable development from her use of imagery and poetic language for its own sake in the early novels to her use of language as a precise instrument of expression in her mature novels. For example, when Clifford is saying good-bye to his wife before he joins the army he caresses a tree in the garden:

"The dear old monkey-puzzle," said Clifford, thoughtlessly caressing it, then cursing as it spiked his hand.
"It's an awful tree," Gwen cried, "I never saw such a beastly tree! I hate it! I loathe it! God, how I'd love to hack it down and watch it bleed."

"Mother loves it," Clifford murmured, looking at his feet. His throat contracted. (p. 30)

In this brief exchange at a moment when Gwen is full of the sorrow of parting from the husband she still loves passionately, the author reveals a basic difference between Clifford and his wife. What he finds attractive and loveable seems to her ugly and hateful. Ultimately because of this difference Gwen destroys Clifford in the way she says she would like to destroy the tree. The harm she does him is later stressed in a conversation with her mother-in-law and sister-in-law after Clifford's death. Both of them blame her for not having warned Clifford in time to prevent the accident which killed him:

"We knew what you were doing to our house"—she gave an odd inflection to the word, as if she meant not merely bricks and mortar but the aristocratic conception of Family—"long before you ... long before he died."

"Your house!" Gwen cried. A tempest of emotion seemed to hurl her body towards them. "I'd like to drag it down on top of the lot of us!"

The room was quiet. The electric fire sparked suddenly and gave out a humming note. Mrs. Burgand fumbled for her sewing, let it slide over the edge of the tray to the floor.

"Isn't that," said Evelyn, "what you've done?" (p. 276)

Here the situation is both completely convincing on a realistic plane and carries metaphoric implications beyond the immediate context.

Another example of the way in which the book gains in depth because of an intermeshing of its literal and metaphoric levels is in the description of two of Gwen's visits to Paul's London practice. On the first occasion Gwen feels the room is ablaze with light and goes "to the fireplace and puts out her hands as if to warm them, before remembering that it was June and the grate was empty. Confused, she straightened up" (p. 231). Her action can be seen as a symbol of her need for Paul's love. She imagines there is a fire burning in his heart for her but in fact he is not in love with her—

the grate is empty and she is left confused. The fire is used as a symbol of her situation again when she pays her final visit to Paul. This time there is a real fire in the grate and sitting in front of it Gwen asks Paul if he has known of her love for him and ever been in love with her. As he begins to answer, "a small green flame sprang up in the heart of the fire. 'Look!' she cried delightedly. He smiled mechanically in admiration. The flame flickered out" (p. 281). Here the flame that suddenly flares into life can be seen as a symbol of Gwen's hope and it dies as her own hope dies when Paul tells her he has never felt more than friendship for her.

Because of the skill with which Pamela Hansford Johnson tells the story, *The Philistines* becomes a very successful and moving study of a young girl's mistake. It creates sympathy for her without obscuring her own responsibility for the situation in which she finds herself. Gwen's unhappy marriage is of her own making, yet the author recognizes her need to break free and find herself. In *Catherine Carter* the young heroine has the same kind of passionate and intelligent nature as Gwen's and makes the same mistake. However, it does not take her as long to free herself, and the emphasis of this book is more on the working out of a successful and enduring relationship between Catherine and the man who becomes her second husband than on the first unsuccessful marriage.

Catherine Carter

Catherine Carter is set in late-nineteenth-century London and its two principal characters are a gifted young actress and a famous actor-manager. Although the setting is completely authentic and Henry Peverel is partly inspired by Sir Henry Irving it would be a mistake to consider it as a novel about the theater. Pamela Hansford Johnson herself points out that it "is not a theatrical biography thinly-veiled: it is a story of the conflict between love and ambition."[5] In it the author takes the opportunity of using the knowledge she gained of Sir Henry Irving's theater through her mother's family, but the book is a study in human relationships remarkably similar to those explored in *The Philistines*. The author suggests it "is a story

of the conflict between love and ambition," but, before Catherine
and Henry fight out their personal battle, Catherine makes an unhappy marriage that has a great deal in common with the unhappy
marriages in both *The Philistines* and *An Impossible Marriage*. It
is only when she has broken free of her first marriage that she is
able to work out a happy marriage with Henry Peverel, the man
who becomes her second husband.

The story is told in a contrapuntal fashion and shows events
alternately from the point of view of the two main characters,
Catherine Carter and Henry Peverel. Catherine, a young girl of
twenty, confident of her gifts as an actress, is auditioned by Victorian London's most famous actor-manager, Henry Peverel, and
given a place in his company at the Belvedere Theatre. It does not
take her long to realize that she is in love with him but his seniority
and fame make her feel he is beyond her reach. Instead she marries
another actor in Peverel's company who flatters her with his attentions—Malcolm Rivers. The son of a baron, Malcolm joined the
theater against his family's wishes and is noted for the single-
minded way in which he pursues what he wants only to lose interest
in it when he has succeeded in making it his own. He is a man of
homosexual tendencies that his mother hopes marriage will inhibit.
Like many of Pamela Hansford Johnson's heroines, Catherine is
born in Clapham, has lost her father at an early age, and lives with
her widowed and dominating mother until she marries. Malcolm
attracts her physically and offers her social status so that she is
tempted to accept his proposal of marriage even though she is
secretly in love with Peverel. It does not take her long to realize her
mistake. Malcolm tires of her soon after she becomes his wife, and
turns instead to his friend Dennis Lane-Belfour, an enterprising
young actor who hopes to manage a theater of his own.

Henry Peverel takes some time to realize that he is in love with
Catherine. He has spent several happy years in love with his leading lady, Isabel Tressall, whose husband, Norbert Philips, is his
musical director. Philips condones his wife's relationship with
Peverel because it offers him a kind of insurance policy. Isabel is
a woman with strong maternal instincts and her passion for Henry

has burnt itself out when the novel opens. She is the one who directs Peverel's attention toward Catherine and persuades him to coach her personally. Once Catherine marries Rivers, the jealousy Henry feels makes him understand the nature of his feelings for her. The opportunity to acknowledge them before her arises when her husband leaves her on the night of her first great triumph in the theater, in order to keep an appointment with Lane-Belfour in Manchester. Catherine is willing to throw caution and discretion to the winds and leave her husband but Henry realizes that for the first time he loves a woman enough to wish to make her his wife. When Malcolm leaves Catherine in London and accepts a place in Dennis Lane-Belfour's company in Manchester, Henry decides to install her in a townhouse of her own.

From the moment that Malcolm leaves Catherine the author concentrates on analyzing the elements that go into the making of an enduring relationship between a man and a woman. Thus the novel goes beyond the portrayal of an impossible marriage to an analysis of the only kind of marriage that is possible. Both Catherine and Henry, who has now been knighted and become sole proprietor of his theater, are ambitious and strong people determined not to be subdued by each other. The struggle between them is actualized by bringing them into conflict on professional matters. Catherine is anxious to persuade Sir Henry to allow her to act as his equal on the stage. All three of the people who are closest to Sir Henry, his secretary, Willy, his former mistress, Isabel, and his wife, Catherine, accuse him of being inclined to surround himself by second-rate talents so that he may shine more brightly. Even though he wishes to make his theater the best theater in London, he hesitates to let his leading lady play against him as a potential rival. Catherine wishes him to stage *Antony and Cleopatra* but he will not agree. The quarrel between them affects their personal relations. She joins the company of Peverel's competitor, Puttock, where she is given the chance of becoming famous in her own right. She remains there until her former husband is given a part to play opposite her and then retires from the stage for a while. Soon afterwards she becomes pregnant. Even during her pregnancy she is restless and longs to return to the stage and when the child dies at birth she withdraws completely from her husband. Peverel understands he has to do something drastic to win her back. He offers her the part of Cleopatra and his concession becomes a victory when he finds he has to assure his wife that she is still capable of acting the part. In spite of a great deal of nervous tension before the first night, Catherine's comeback as Cleopatra is a triumph and she and her husband stand as equals on the stage. The equality that they achieve on stage reflects the equality they have achieved as man and wife. After many crises, struggles of will, and compromises, the two of them have arrived at the kind of union that will endure.

In this novel Pamela Hansford Johnson has created a gallery full of memorable characters. Henry Peverel and Catherine Carter are shown from several points of view. Their own thoughts and feelings, their view of each other and the views of the people who surround them all coalesce to give the impression of fully rounded persons.

In addition to these two major figures, the character of Peverel's lifelong companion, Willy Palliser, is developed in considerable depth. He knows Peverel better than anyone else and has a certain pride in this knowledge. On one level he is dominated by Henry and allows him to make the decisions, on another he is something of a mischief-maker who cannot resist manipulating people. He wishes to befriend Catherine but cannot help being jealous of her closeness to his friend and mentor. Catherine frequently feels annoyed with him but eventually comes to understand him.

Isabel Tressall, Henry's mistress, is also created with meticulous care. Her love of Henry, her interest in Catherine, her instinctive wisdom, and her indulgent affection for her husband and children are gradually unfolded to reveal a fully rounded character. Catherine's mother, the "little General," is another successful character with her interfering love for Catherine and her ability to make her daughter extremely embarrassed at the same time as she can suddenly prove unexpectedly understanding and perceptive. Even Dennis Lane-Belfour, Malcolm Rivers's friend, is completely convincing, an unashamed opportunist who has a genius for introducing changes in the theater that will bear fruit in the twentieth century.

The narrative flows with considerable ease. The novel is divided into three parts and the chapters in each are very brief. The author is content to make one main point in each and thus explores the relationships involved. From time to time she does not hesitate to intrude with an authorial comment. For example, Catherine goes to Venice in the hope of forcing Henry Peverel's hand. She is convinced that he will be unable to stop himself from pursuing her and declaring his love. While she waits there she spends her days sight-seeing and the writer is able to comment on her emotional state and explain the lessons life is teaching her: "So, in the church of S. Giovanni e Paolo, Catherine received her first intimation of the greatest function of human love, which is to enable men and women simultaneously to desire and to possess" (p. 286). A similar reflection on the nature of love is made when Catherine suddenly finds that for three days she is able to look at Henry "without love or illusion" (p. 349). Later the writer explains the value of the lesson this break in love has taught her: "It was a comfort to her, for it had one lasting effect: it had destroyed the more bizarre impulses of jealousy. She would be jealous of him again, and often; but because she had been able to see him, for those three days, as a man among other men, proportioned to the natural world, not merely as some phenomenal creature made out of her own light, her jealousy would from now on be a sane one, freed of ugliness and nightmare and the obsessive greed of the heart" (p. 351). These philosophic comments enrich the story with a moral perspective that lifts *Catherine Carter* above the level of a conventional love story. Walter Allen speaks of "Miss Hansford Johnson's skill in rendering the complexities, the contradictions, the discontinuities of behavior, so that in the end the action she described could stand as a satisfying image of life itself, one rendered with a sad, lucid, honest acceptance that made it not silly to be reminded of George Eliot."[6] Although Walter Allen has *The Last Resort* in mind, his judgement can be applied equally to *Catherine Carter*. The name of George Eliot springs readily to mind largely because both these authors are seriously concerned with the moral issues involved in human relationships and because of the similarity of their use of the author's voice for moral reflection.

An Impossible Marriage

An Impossible Marriage is more like *The Philistines* than either of them is like *Catherine Carter* because the fact that the latter novel is set in the Victorian theater world gives it a glamour that is absent from the dull suburban world in which the heroines of the other two books have to live their lives.

Christine Jackson, the protagonist of *An Impossible Marriage*, is one of Pamela Hansford Johnson's admitted attempts at a self-portrait. The basic facts have been used in earlier portraits like that of Mary Captor in *The Monument*, and in the case of both Gwen and Catherine, although Gwen's gifts were confined mainly to the reading of books and Catherine's artistic talents found expression on the stage. Nevertheless the situation of a gifted young woman who loses her father at an early age and grows up living in close contact with a strong-minded mother or mother-substitute is used sufficiently frequently in Johnson's fiction to draw attention as a recurrent pattern.

The story of Christine's mistake is rapidly told. As a young girl one of her closest friends, Iris Allbright, was attractive and flirtatious enough to make Christine feel downright plain. When she attends a dance in Iris's company and meets Ned Skelton, at least ten years her senior, she falls passionately in love with him. While they are courting, several incidents make Christine aware of Ned's failings but she cannot resist when he rushes her into an engagement. After their engagement, Ned's mother's constant criticism of her son's character and Christine's realization that he has considerable experience with other women, make her realize that they will not be happy together. Just when Christine is about to break off her engagement, Iris appears like an evil *deus ex machina* and, by threatening to steal Ned, makes him desirable once more. After their marriage it does not take long for Christine to realize that she finds it impossible. Ned is a failure as a breadwinner and becomes increasingly moody and quarrelsome. For a time Christine is absorbed in caring for her son, Mark, but Ned is jealous of the child and the tension between them increases. Christine begins to plead for a divorce and after steadily refusing her Ned suddenly gives in. It takes Christine twenty years to find out why. As a successful writer happily married for the second time she returns to the scene of her childhood in order to face her friend (and personal demon) Iris. Iris tells Christine what she herself has only just found out, that Ned agreed to divorce her because he had been unfaithful to her. On the occasion that he went away to play golf with a friend, he met Caroline, one of Christine's old friends, who was herself divorced and lonely. Knowing that Christine no longer wanted Ned, Caroline agreed to sleep with him. As long as Ned had remained faithful to Christine he had felt justified in refusing to divorce her, but once he knew of his own infidelity he felt he had no choice but to agree. Having found out the truth Christine feels released from the burden of the past and is able to go forth a free woman: "A stranger there myself, I was free" (p. 344).

As a reviewer of this book points out, "baldly stated, a resumé is of little service to this novel; its strength lies in the qualities which illuminate its development."[7] One of its special qualities is the way in which Johnson uses the device of the narrator. In the same way as Claud looked back on his first romantic love, in *Too Dear for My Possessing*, Christine Jackson looks back on her own past and tells her own story. The mature and happy older woman can thus comment philosophically on the girl she once was. At the same time references to the happiness she has subsequently found contrast with her earlier misery.

As in the case of *Too Dear for My Possessing*, the influence of Proust is apparent in the significance that is attached to the past and to memory. A passage from *Remembrance of Things Past* (which according to Pamela Hansford Johnson should have been translated *In Search of Lost Time*[8]) that is quoted on the title page draws attention to the theme of "lost time." As Christine stands at "the closed door" steeling herself to see Iris again she writes in a way that deliberately echoes Proust: "I do not like looking back down the chasm of the past and seeing, in a moment of vertigo, some terror that looks like a joy, some joy crouched like a terror. It is better to keep one's eyes on the rock-face of the present, for that is real; what is under your nose is actual, but the past is full of lies, and the only accurate memories are those we refuse to admit to our consciousness."[9] The use of the word vertigo echoes two lines in the paragraph quoted from Proust, *"J'étais juché à son sommet vertigineux"* and *"J'avais le vertige de voir au-dessous de moi,"* and is repeated toward the end of the book when, after her confrontation with Iris, Christine confesses that she never found out what made her husband change his mind so suddenly about agreeing to divorce her. Iris knows the answer and is prepared to tell Christine, who feels suddenly afraid: "She was forcing me to look behind, to look down the vertiginous fall of the years" (p. 340). But, contrary to her expectations, confronting the past makes her free of it.

Echoes of Proust can also be heard in Christine's thoughts as she leaves Iris's home. She realizes that she will not visit Iris again in spite of her request that she do so, because she fears "the yesterday she bore with her as inseparably as her own shadow" (p. 343). The epigraph from Proust has the same idea: *"Je ne pouvais me mouvoir sans le déplacer avec moi"* (I cannot move without taking it with me). Significantly, when Christine leaves Iris's flat and walks through Clapham, which she has known so well and where all the events recounted have taken place, she sees a boy who reminds her of her old friend Dicky: "It was so like Dicky as he used to be that for a moment I was almost recaptured by time; but then he dismounted to speak to a girl, and his voice was a stranger's" (p. 344). Thus Christine's enforced journey into her own past makes her realize that the person she once was is a stranger to her present self and that "we must live in the present if we are to remain real; not to ourselves, but to other people about us" (p. 343). The theme of lost time that is thus sounded gives the subject of an impossible marriage an added dimension in this book. The difficulties of the relationship between Christine and Ned are fully explored and the entire experience, even though it is a painful one, is related to the question of Christine's moral growth.

General Discussion

One of the striking things about Pamela Hansford Johnson's treatment of the subject of marriage in all three books is the way she includes a full picture of the families involved. Gwen and Clifford, Catherine and Malcolm Rivers, Christine and Ned do not exist in isolation, they come from a definite background which is part of what they are and have other family ties and loyalties. The mother figure in each one of the novels is extremely dominant. Mrs. Burgand contributes greatly to the problems that Gwen has to face as Clifford's wife and Lady Lalage Rivers is an equally important figure in Catherine's marriage. Catherine's own mother also plays an important part in her daughter's relationship with both Malcolm and Henry, and in *An Impossible Marriage,* Aunt Emilie, whom her father married after the death of Christine's mother, places heavy demands on Christine's conscience by making her feel guilty for leaving her alone when she marries and not yielding to the pressure of her desire to make her home with Christine.

The author is also remarkable in that she does not hesitate to treat the subject of sexual desire and fulfillment in women. All three of her heroines find out that marriage awakens their sexuality and they are capable of great physical joy. Yet in spite of having found partners to whom they are strongly attracted they learn that intellectual compatibility does not automatically follow. Often, physical pleasure is all that they have left in common with their husbands. A. S. Byatt observes that "Pamela Hansford Johnson is one of the very few living (or dead) women novelists who is able to describe sexual happiness in women with interest or conviction."[10] This is noticeably true. Not only does she describe sexual happiness, but she describes sexual longing and frustration in women as well. She is also rare in that she includes the experiences of child-bearing and motherhood within a marriage. This would seem an essential part of the subject, yet even today there are comparatively few novelists who include these aspects of woman's experience. Catherine's depression when she loses her baby, Christine's experience of labor, the effect of tension and worry on her ability to feed her son, and the jealousy that Ned feels when his wife devotes herself to his child are all part of the experience of marriage and the novelist's inclusion of these aspects makes the marriages that she describes firmly rooted in a recognizable reality.

Whereas the problems of the world at large usually play an important part in Johnson's fiction, these novels are primarily studies in individual relationships, and outside matters are only briefly mentioned. Gwen quarrels with Clifford's mother and sister when they are pleased about Munich and believe England has been saved from war (p. 24). Catherine shows a flash of social conscience when she sees a beggar (p. 372), and Christine's old friend, a Jewish boy nicknamed "Take Plato," returns from a trip to Germany and tells her about the persecution of the Jews, saying that he worries about the "state of the world" (pp. 302–303). These examples of the author's interest in world affairs would pass unnoticed if it were not for the persistence of her efforts to weave them into so many of the other books she has written. In these books any effort to make more of them would give the impression that the author was trying too hard to enlarge her canvas. Indeed Marianne Hauser correctly points out in her review of *Too Dear for My Possessing* that the author has failed to establish a "connection between the plot and world events" yet clearly feels "uneasy about discussing love instead of politics."[11] She has avoided making the same mistake in these novels. By withstanding the temptation to introduce these world events and politics arbitrarily, and by choosing to concentrate upon exploring the most basic of human institutions, she has acquired a depth and moral seriousness that endow the individual case with universality.

Chapter Eight

Love and Renunciation

The moral seriousness which is evident in Pamela Hansford Johnson's treatment of marriage in the novels discussed in the previous chapter is focused on a specific moral problem in the two novels to be discussed here. *The Last Resort* (1956) and *The Humbler Creation* (1959) treat, in their different ways, one of the central conflicts in the "great tradition" of the English novel—the conflict between love and duty. In *The Last Resort* Eric Aveling discovers that his own moral fastidiousness prevents him from finding happiness with the woman he loves even though the death of his wife has left him legally free to do so. Similarly in *The Humbler Creation* the vicar of a London parish realizes that his sense of moral responsibility is too strong to make it possible for him to leave his wife, although she is frigid and he has fallen deeply in love with another woman.

As Susan M. Black points out in her review of *The Humbler Creation* it is not very fashionable today to write about "the human heart in conflict," yet great writers like Faulkner maintain that these problems are the only ones worth writing about.[1] In both these novels Johnson treats the "old-fashioned" theme in a modern context. Her protagonists know that their society claims to have jettisoned the moral values that continue to govern their own conduct. The fact that their dilemma still has a great deal of relevance is demonstrated by the way in which several leading critics have praised these particular novels. Walter Allen, for example, feels that *The Last Resort* is "one of the best novels of our time."[2] John

Gardner's recent book *On Moral Fiction* is a sign of a reversal of the trend to estimate innovation in the novel more highly than its traditional use as a medium for the analysis and search for human values.[3] If his pleas win ground, then Gerald Sykes's forecast that *The Humbler Creation* "is going to enter the small pantheon of the significant books of our day" will certainly prove true.[4]

The Last Resort

The story of *The Last Resort* is told by a novelist-narrator, Christine Hall, whom the reader recognizes as the narrator of *An Impossible Marriage*. Since both novels have the same narrator it would seem logical to treat them together, but in fact the difference in theme makes it easier to treat them apart. In *An Impossible Marriage* Christine is telling a story in which she herself is the protagonist and she tells it in order to show how a relationship between two people can disintegrate. In *The Last Resort* she is a sympathetic observer and the emphasis is placed on the pain of losing a person who is still beloved.

The Last Resort opens with the meeting between Christine and Celia Baird, an acquaintance who rapidly makes a confidante of Christine. Celia is in love with an old family friend, Eric Aveling, whose wife, Lois, is dying slowly of an incurable disease at a hospital not far from the seaside hotel where Celia's parents live. Eric and Celia are not conventionally moral in that they both feel free to become lovers as long as they do not hurt Lois for whom they both care. It is Celia's mother who deliberately destroys her daughter's chance of happiness by making sure that Lois guesses that Eric is in love with Celia. Deeply hurt, Lois revenges herself by confronting Eric with her knowledge just before she dies, thereby loading him with a burden of guilt that makes it impossible for him to continue his relationship with Celia after Lois's death. Eric succeeds in making a new life for himself by marrying Nancy Sheriff, the charming young daughter of an impoverished aristocrat whom his partner, Junius Evans, has deliberately thrown in his way. Celia's facade of acceptance breaks down when she learns that

Nancy is going to bear Eric a child. Ultimately she is left completely alone. Her possessive mother dies, her father rejects her offer to come and take care of him and finally Celia decides to marry Junius who is known to be a homosexual. Junius has been deserted by the young man he loves and so the two frustrated and lonely people try to find consolation with each other.

Although this novel is not divided into formal parts in the way that many of Pamela Hansford Johnson's novels are, it has a clear four-part structure. The first part shows Christine's meeting with Celia and the way she learns about Celia and Eric's love for each other. It ends with Christine's return to London. In the second part Christine's absorption with her own life is counterpointed with Celia's life in London where she runs a typing agency and frequents dubious nightclubs. Christine sees her delight in these "dreary squanderings" as a refuge: "She needed, if ever she should be made desolate, to have something of her own."[5]

The third part is the longest and describes the painful dissolution of the relationship between Eric and Celia after Lois's death. By this time Eric and his partner Junius have also learned to confide in Christine so that their points of view can be presented through her. Eric's marriage brings this section to a close and the fourth part shows Celia left without anyone to care for until her decision to marry Junius which Christine sees as an attempt to find "some kind of country she could call her own" (p. 298).

Even this brief synopsis should make it clear that the moral problem is a complex one. Eric and Celia feel it is better to deceive Lois than to hurt her, but Eric finds it better to hurt Celia than to live with her and feel guilty. No definitive judgements are made but events are colored by Christine's view of them and of the people involved.

In her review of *The Last Resort*, Elizabeth Janeway is critical of Pamela Hansford Johnson's choice of Christine as a narrator: "Celia's history is narrated by that troublesome, ubiquitous, 'old friend' who infests English fiction of the middle range, the 'I' who is an observer but not a participant. . . . The tidy narrator is unimportant as a person; but as a device she thoroughly hampers the story, for she not only forces it one remove away from the reader. She also narrows the range it can move through to what is seen by one pair of eyes, and to a rather narrow, reportorial realism."[6] The question why Johnson (with the degree of professional competence she had acquired when she wrote this novel) should deliberately choose to sacrifice the "immediacy of feeling'" Elizabeth Janeway misses is worth raising. A. S. Byatt, admittedly English and therefore perhaps inclined to tolerate the use of the device, actually praises Johnson's use of a narrator: *"The Last Resort* is so good partly because the sexually happy novelist and the created heroine in pain are both real, and the novelist's curiosity is part of the plot and focus for it."[7] Although any judgment on such an issue will inevitably be subjective, it is important to notice what is gained by the use of an objective narrator. Christine's happy and fulfilled life acts as a foil to Celia's miserable and frustrated one. Christine is also able to present Junius and Eric's point of view as distinct from Celia's. Above all she is able to analyze the wider moral implications of the individual case, thereby adding that "sad, lucid, honest acceptance" of life that reminds Walter Allen of George Eliot.[8]

Christine is often critical of Celia, noting her faults and drawing attention to the way unhappiness makes her more and more like her mother. At the same time she relates Celia's suffering to the question of martyrdom. At first she considers that Celia has the ability to "make and keep resolutions which must change a whole life: a member of that most incomprehensible of companies, in which are the martyrs and the saints" (p. 189). But when Celia breaks down and gives her agony full expression Christine realizes she has been mistaken and that "Celia had not been able to make that muscling leap of the nerves which turns the human being into the saint" (p. 236). This way of correcting her opinions as events prove her wrong enhances the impression of her reliability as a narrator. It is only because of Christine's interpretation of the motives behind Celia's marriage to Junius that the reader accepts it as more than a contrivance of the plot:

She would do her best for Junius in gratitude, perhaps, for the sin from which he was inadvertently to save her. Celia believed in sin; it had always been inseparable in her mind from her love for Aveling. If she had married him it would have been a taint behind their lives, recognised by them both. Neither of them had been able to escape from the Puritanism deep in their natures. I remembered what he had said to me several years ago, in the road beyond the ugly hospital where Lois lay dying.

"Underneath it all is the undertow of the Ten Commandments. They make dreadful fools of us. They're like our grandmother's sideboard, which we don't use anymore, but can't bring ourselves to sell. There it is all the time, weighing us down from the attic or biding its time in the cellar."

In this strange and empty marriage there would be no sin for Celia. If she suffered through it she would have the consolation (of inestimable worth to one of her temperament) of knowing that this suffering was not a punishment for wrong-doing. Her conscience would be clear. (p. 284)

In this passage Christine is not only presenting a convincing explanation of Celia's behavior but also defining the nature of the moral problem. For people like Eric and Celia, however free they might imagine themselves to be from conventional rules of sexual morality, cannot live with a guilty conscience whatever the cost in emotional terms. Thus in the end Christine has to revise her opinion yet again and recognize Celia as a latter-day martyr. In this respect Celia knows herself better than Christine does. Just before her marriage, in a revealing conversation with her friend she says, "But I can walk on the waters" (p. 286), thus placing herself in the company of no less a martyr than Jesus himself.

The American title, *The Sea and the Wedding*, is quite different from the English one. Both titles have a similar meaning and are clarified in the conversation just quoted. In order to explain the title it is necessary to repeat a somewhat longer passage. The sea along which Celia and Christine take many walks is a symbol of freedom for Celia. On an appropriately stormy and bleak day the two friends go out for a last walk together:

"Not inspiriting," said Celia.

I said that any resort looked desolate out of season.

"Sometimes I think this is the last resort." She smiled sourly. "I don't think I could have stuck the Moray for so long if it hadn't been for the sea. It gives me a sense of freedom."

I replied that it gave me a sense of being shut in: I did not like to feel there was one direction in which I could not walk.

"Oh, but I can walk on the waters," said Celia, "when people madden me. I can go out and out, right over there, and disappear entirely from the view." (p. 286)

This conversation makes it clear that Celia's marriage to Junius is her last resort and that the sea, which stands for freedom, is opposed to the wedding, which shuts her in. Incidentally, the difference between Celia and Christine's attitude toward the sea is an effective way of underlining the difference between their way of looking at things. Christine is satisfied with the life she has and has no need to walk away from it, whereas Celia has to look out away from her world toward the sea to gain a sense of freedom from the bondage her life becomes.

One of the strengths of this novel is the way in which the author concentrates upon comparatively few characters and makes each one fully convincing. Celia's father, Dr. Baird, is especially noteworthy as one of the few strong fathers in Pamela Hansford Johnson's work. Usually the mothers are widowed or married to weak men whom they dominate, but in this novel the pattern is reversed. Celia's mother is the weaker partner, and Dr. Baird is aggressive and sharp-tongued. Yet, in spite of his alarming manner, there seems to exist a bond of genuine affection between him and his daughter. Celia's mother is possessive and selfish in the tradition of the worst mothers in Johnson's fiction. Unhappy in her own marriage—the first thing that Christine notices is the way husband and wife sit on the sofa with a "space between them"—she fills the gap in her emotional life by placing heavy demands on her daughter.

Junius, Eric's homosexual partner, is a complex personality cast in the same mold as Willy Palliser in *Catherine Carter*. Through him Johnson explores ideas she has shown an interest in earlier. The intensity of the feelings that can exist between people of the same sex is a subject that recurs in her work and is present in her first novel, *This Bed Thy Centre*, where Elsie is plagued by her love for her teacher Leda Chevasse. There are also a couple of homosexual actors in *The Trojan Brothers* and in the same novel the relationship between Sid and his partner Benny is so deep as to verge on homosexuality—they joke about being taken for "pansies." In *Catherine Carter* the bond between Henry Peverel and Willy is similar in nature and homosexuality is overtly treated in Malcolm Rivers's relationship with Dennis Lane-Belfour. In *The Last Resort* Junius's feelings are frequently analyzed from his own point of view in a way that conveys the intensity of his pain.

A trait in Junius's character which is noticeable as a characteristic of several other characters Johnson has created is his tendency to cast himself in a variety of parts and to play them accordingly. The author first used this characteristic in her description of Claud's father, Richard Pickering, in *Too Dear for My Possessing*, and it comes back again in Leslie, the young boy whom Christine dated before she married Ned in *An Impossible Marriage*. It is treated most fully as an aspect of the personality of Henry Peverel in *Catherine Carter*, a man who is so much the actor that he finds himself playing a part even when he wishes to be most himself. Similarly Junius is always acting so that it is difficult for Christine to know when he is being sincere.

In *The Last Resort* many of the details recall other novels. An idea that Johnson uses in this novel and in many of her previous ones is the way in which people fall in love with the image of a person that they have created for themselves rather than with the person as he really is. This idea is the subject of a whole chapter in *Catherine Carter* when Catherine suddenly sees Henry Peverel without the mask of love, but it is suggested much earlier in the story of Claud's love for Cecil (*Too Dear for My Possessing*) and also analyzed negatively through Sid's inability to develop an image of Anna when she is not there (*The Trojan Brothers*). In *The Last Resort*, Christine notices how Celia has "to hide continually behind the image her mother had made of her" (p. 61) and later when Nancy confesses her fear that her husband may fall in love with Celia once more Christine reflects that

nothing was so completely destroyed by time as a love affair of the past. Sometimes, I thought to myself, one fantasticated it, believed that if the once-beloved object were to reappear all would begin over again: but believed wrongly. It did not matter so much that time altered people. What did matter was that it altered our idea of them. They became, in the moment of our love, what they could never be again once the gauze of that love had been withdrawn from them. They were just men and women, flesh and blood, a pimple at the lip, a vein in an eye-ball, a broken finger-nail, a loosened muscle, a smile too short, a stare too long. For we did not love men and women, but only the angels we made of them. (p. 241)

Even in her response to Junius, whom she dislikes when she first meets him, Christine reveals the same basic idea: "I did not think round and about him at all, as one thinks of individuals, winding them in a cocoon of memory, speculation, opinion" (p. 80). It is only when Junius helps her through a crisis that Christine suddenly realizes that she is seeing him clearly as a person for the first time (p. 83).

In *The Last Resort*, Johnson also makes a good deal of use of a device that she uses often and most noticeably in the Helena trilogy. People are often described in comparison to figures in paintings. Eric, for example, reminds Christine of Velasquez's paintings: "His body had a disjointed air that I associated vaguely with grandeur; Velasquez often disjointed a king at the elbow or the knee" (p. 33). A couple of prostitutes whom Christine and Celia see on an evening walk through Park Lane are "like figures by Chirico" (p. 218) and Nancy is "like a Rubens woman incongruously gifted with the power of reflection" (p. 240). This habit of seeing things with the painter's eye is especially characteristic of Pamela Hansford Johnson's style.

On the other hand, the interest in outside events that is so marked in many of the earlier novels is reduced to a minimum in a novel

like *The Last Resort*, where the emphasis is clearly on human relationships. Even so, a few revealing references are included. Celia
and Christine are "veterans of the Spanish War" and have carried
banners in the 1930s (p. 14). Dr. Baird is an old reactionary who
enjoys discussing politics with Christine's more liberal husband.
Eric teases Nancy for being a snob but she is more radical than her
husband.

The social group from which the people in this novel are drawn
is comparatively rare in Pamela Hansford Johnson's fiction. Here she
deals with the upper middle and upper class, not with what Jo in
The Survival of the Fittest aptly labeled the "middle-middle" class.
Although Christine herself comes from this group—in *An Impossible Marriage* she says she comes not from the lower-middle or
from the upper-middle but from a class almost equidistant from the
two (p. 106)—she moves in a more privileged group. Celia is remarkably well-to-do and loves spending money. Lois is also extremely wealthy and sets Eric up with his own firm of architects
after their marriage. Nancy's father is an aristocrat, albeit an impoverished one, and his brother is both affluent and influential.
Junius is a social climber who makes the reader well aware of the
importance of position and social status in the world he inhabits.
This world, with its expensive seaside hotels, apartments near Hyde
Park, and nightclubs in Soho, is a far cry from Clapham Common
and the shabby suburbs of the earlier novels.

The Humbler Creation

The theme of the renunciation of love is more sharply defined
in *The Humbler Creation* than in *The Last Resort* because the protagonist is the man who has to make the decision to renounce rather
than the woman who has to suffer the agony of being renounced.
The conflict between love and duty in this novel is also complicated
by the fact that Maurice Fisher is the vicar of his parish and therefore a representative of the Church at a time when that institution
is especially vulnerable because so few people believe in it.

Maurice Fisher is a profoundly passionate and a profoundly

religious man. Unfortunately he has always found that "sex was too like sin to be comfortable" and his marriage to a beautiful but frigid woman augments his sense of guilt.[9] When the novel opens Maurice's temporary liberation from the burden of responsibility toward his wife, Libby, her mother, Mrs. Marsden, her widowed sister, Kate, and Kate's two sons, Simon and Dick, makes him realize how much he enjoys being on his own. The unexpected return of the family from their seaside holiday floods him with a sense of disappointment that foreshadows the development of the entire story. For a brief time Maurice will enjoy the illusion of freedom to love another woman but the demands of his family will imprison him once more. The story is a simple one but it has a few unusual facets. Libby is a remarkably beautiful but hopelessly inadequate woman who has "succeeded in fooling nearly all the people all of the time" into thinking of her as the ideal vicar's wife (p. 237). Her sister, Kate, is everything that she is not, and acts as the vicar's "refuge and strength" (p. 9). Kate's affection for her brother-in-law is so strong as to border on love, yet she is the one to force him to make the ultimate sacrifice. Maurice's real reason for giving up Alice Imber, with whom he falls deeply in love, is not submission to the call of duty to the Church but recognition of his responsibility toward Libby and her mother, once Kate has made it clear that she no longer intends to share his burden. Ironically enough, Kate's reason for forcing the vicar to do his duty is her own love for a derelict journalist—a love that is manifestly less "worthy" than the vicar's love for Alice. Yet paradoxically it proves that once he has made the conventionally "right" decision for the "wrong" reasons he feels closer to God and finds peace (p. 343).

Both Maurice and Alice have a strong sense of guilt, and although they are not technically guilty of adultery they realize that the mere fact of their deep love for each other is a betrayal. Libby makes Maurice realize this when she tells him that she cares less for the fact that he has not slept with Alice than for the fact that he has "given her everything I care about" (p. 258). One of Alice's oldest friends, Reginald Plymmer, tells her the same thing: "'Did you suppose I was committing adultery?' she asked. 'Oh, don't try to fool your Uncle Reginald,' he said, with sudden savage vulgarity, 'I believe it's all bee-ewtiful, all up in the head. But you're committing it all right, and the mess you're making is nobody's business'" (p. 291).

When Maurice feels that he cannot bear to give Alice up she tells him of the way in which Libby has come to see her and made her squirm with guilt (p. 294). Ultimately, when Maurice comes to take his farewell of her, Alice finds it easier to bear the thought of losing him than of feeling guilty: "It will mean that I am not doing wrong for once. And if I can face this decently I may be forgiven some of the other things. It is curious that though I cannot believe in God, I am continually aware of the presence of some spiritual book-keeper with a profit-and-loss account" (p. 341). What Alice says is rather similar to what Eric said in *The Last Resort* about the "undertow of the Ten Commandments." Even though Alice does not believe in religion she finds herself impelled to live by its rules. Maurice, too, finds that though he does not approve of the disciplinary approach to religion that is voiced by one of the members of the Parochial Church Council, George Kitson, it contains a core of hard truth: "The Church held the only set of rules for most men to live by; and it was vital that the hand which held them should be a trusted one" (pp. 334–35).

Maurice and Alice's unhappy love story is juxtaposed to Kate's "happy" one with considerable effect. Kate and Alice are rather alike, both religious skeptics, both widowed and both capable in a way that shows up Libby's inability to cope. Their loves are very different, however. The love between Alice and Maurice is based on considerable intellectual rapport. The two of them can talk to each other and refrain from the physical expression of their love. The essence of Kate's passion is sensual. Tom Westlake is an out-of-work alcoholic married to a Roman Catholic wife who only agrees to divorce him when she finds a lover of her own. Tom's lack of moral fiber is brought out in the incident where he allows Kate to perjure herself in court in order to save him from a charge for drunken driving that will cost him his licence. Then he leaves her to suffer because she has made him lose his self-respect. When Kate agrees to marry him she does so knowing that her sons will never accept him and that she will deprive Maurice of all hope of leaving Libby. The very ruthlessness of her determination to find her own happiness at all costs makes Maurice's act of sacrifice seem greater.

The relationship between two homosexuals, Peter and Lou, is an additional contrast to the vicar's story. Peter and Lou live together, flouting convention. Soon after his meeting with Kate in Cambridge the vicar is recalled to his parish, and one of his visitors is Peter. When Peter tells Maurice he has come to a difficult decision he presumes that he and Lou have decided to live separately: "He waited for the news of the renunciation; and was touched by pity. . . . He was touched by the cheerfulness with which Peter came with his sacrifice; it was the kind of bravery Maurice had always admired in others and had hoped to find in himself, if the need for it should ever come to him" (p. 150). In actual fact Peter has not come to renounce his love but to ask for a share in the work of the parish which the vicar is forced to refuse because the Church will not condone homosexuality. The fact that their relationship excludes them from participating in the spiritual life of the parish and the way in which Maurice admires them when he thinks they are going to sacrifice their relationship relates their situation to Maurice's and foreshadows his own act of renunciation.

Like Celia in *The Last Resort*, Maurice belongs to the company of saints and martyrs. The title alludes to a well-known hymn which is being sung in the church when Alice goes there full of the misery of her hopeless love (p. 156). It is given a special meaning toward the end of the novel when Maurice sits down and reads about the martyrdom of Thomas Hawkes: "Maurice thought that a man like himself, so much more obviously of the humbler creation, was a small creature to a man like this; and that what he had to offer was little enough" (p. 345). His sacrifice of the love he feels for Alice can thus be seen as the necessary agony of the true man of God. In his review of this book John Coleman suggests that "Fisher is diminished by it, a man looking at the night sky and saying 'I am a speck to that.' "[10] Granville Hicks on the other hand feels that "the renunciation with which the book ends is moving" and that "neither he nor we have any doubt of the magnitude of his ordeal."[11] It can hardly be denied that the author intends Maurice's gesture to be magnified rather than diminished by the comparison to a historical martyr and to show that in their own humble way people are still willing to suffer for the sake of their beliefs: "Thy humbler creation though feeble their lays with true adoration shall sing to thy praise" (p. 156). Maurice's martryrdom is not spectacular, but it is infinitely real.

Even though the parish of St. Lawrence's is in a big city like London, Pamela Hansford Johnson shows how the boroughs of London are more like a conglomeration of small villages and do not offer the anonymity of the big city. The parish of St. Lawrence's Church near Vernon Square consists of a small number of believers, but they are fighting for survival in a world that threatens their existence. The true values of the community are brought out by bringing together the parishioners in the course of their group activities—the youth club, the meetings of the church council, amateur theatricals, and church bazaars. The people who are happily married, like the old couple Humphery and Georgina Pelham and Colonel Johnson-Black and his wife, Joan, are the ones who are most sympathetic to the troubles of their fellows and show the true Christian spirit. Others, who have suffered unhappiness themselves, like Reginald Plymmer, or who are less certain of the basis of their own marriages, like Jeremy Fawcett and his wife, Louisa, are far quicker to condemn the vicar and insist that appearances must be maintained.

One of the reasons why this novel is completely convincing is that the author allows crises to arise out of comparatively trivial everyday incidents rather than out of unusual events. Thus Maurice realizes that something is wrong by the way the members of his youth club keep giggling at him. Libby realizes with a shock that her husband has stopped loving her when he speaks irritably to her in front of a dinner guest. Alice knows Maurice loves her when he tells her he is going to spend a day in Cambridge and asks her if she will be there, and the sermon that Maurice's well-meaning curate gives on the text of "Judge not, that ye be not judged" brings matters to a head and forces Kitson to inform the bishop. Maurice's realization that he will have to endure life with Libby comes to him without words when Kate announces her decision to marry Tom.

In her characteristic manner, Pamela Hansford Johnson counterpoints several points of view. Maurice, Alice, Libby, Kate, and several of the minor characters are all shown as thinking and feeling individuals, and sometimes the same event is told first as experienced by one and then by the other. Thus, for example, the incident when Maurice is prevented from keeping an appointment with Alice is first told from his point of view and then is retold from the point of view of Alice's sitting and waiting for him to come and after a great deal of mental agony going to her phone and discovering it is dead.

In this novel Johnson uses symbols and images very sparingly and to great effect. One such image is that of the spire of the Church of St. Lawrence's, which is still lopped as the result of a precaution against bombing taken fifteen years ago (p. 5). Once Maurice has carried out his decision to give up Alice he walks to the church and sees the spire: "The chopped spire was ugly in its mutilation, it looked defeated. They will have to restore it. Kitson will have to get on to them about it" (p. 342). Without being exaggeratedly Freudian it is justifiable to identify the frustrated vicar with his mutilated church. He too is defeated like the spire and he too has to be restored, and it is Kitson, with his "disciplinary religion," who is most likely to see that is done.

The way in which Johnson uses color and light symbolically has already been noticed by Susan M. Black, who is worth quoting on the subject:

The author writes of skies that are transparent, violet, cobalt, brilliant with stars and lime-green. She described [sic] blazes, bubbles, gleams and lozenges of light that may be pale, deforming, dull, reflected, lemon, sallow, torporous or sour and that comes from fire, lamp, sun and moon. Characters radiate light figuratively: there's the "so inhumanly bright" assistant vicar whose romance "suffered from the limelight of a parish" and who was wont to send "an azure gleam of amusement in Maurice's direction." Fisher's principles are "illuminating," Libby "glows" only at bazaars and as Alice's father-in-law lies dying in "moneyed brightness" the author takes us into the "stained-glass windows of his mind." Alice's room is literally and symbolically the brightest spot in the book. Maurice comes to adore the light she is so fond of. [12]

The use of light is not, however, equated in a simple way with happiness or joy. For example, when the vicar has been looking forward to going home to a meal on his own and a comfortable evening by the fire with a book he is "drenched" with disappointment to find his house "blazing with light" as a sign of his family's return (pp. 6–7). Similarly the light in Alice's room gives a false impression of happiness to an outsider when Maurice is there saying good-bye to her: "Someone in the street outside might be looking up at the glowing window, envying the happiness that he fancied lay behind it" (p. 349). The brightness in Alice's room is also a threat to Libby, who is dazzled by it when she comes to confront her: "So this was where he came, into this smart, bright place, into this room of light colours only the childless rich could afford" (p. 286). The first time that Maurice's curate meets Alice even though he likes her he feels that she is a threat to his world: "For no reason that he could understand, even though she attracted him, even though he felt that she was good, she threatened to make a crack in the familiar, comfortable and shabby wall of their lives" (p. 43). Through her complex use of light in association with Alice the author shows how she is both an attraction and a threat. The last thing that Maurice does is to go upstairs to Libby and put out the light and it is in his strength to do this that his virtue lies.

One of the few negative reviews of this novel appeared in the *Times Literary Supplement*, where the critic feels that the novel fails because the theme "calls for resources of passionate rhetoric which the author lacks."[13] This objection is similar to the one expressed by Elizabeth Janeway in regard to *The Last Resort* about a lack of immediacy of feeling. It seems to me that the muted key in which the whole novel is written makes the story so much more real and fits in well with the overall concept of the feebleness of the efforts of humble people to remain virtuous according to their lights while showing that out of such material true martyrs are made.

Chapter Nine

The "Dorothy Merlin Comedies"

A group of three satirical novels that differ in tone and type from the rest of Pamela Hansford Johnson's fiction are referred to by the author as the "Dorothy Merlin Comedies," even though Dorothy Merlin is not the protagonist of any one of the three.[1] However, the playwright Dorothy Merlin and her group of friends appear in all three books and it is convenient to use the common label.

The Unspeakable Skipton

The first of these three novels, *The Unspeakable Skipton* (1959), attracted more notice than any of the author's books since *This Bed Thy Centre*. Critics were impressed by her ability to write a successful comic novel so different from her previous work. Several leading periodicals published long reviews that included an appraisal of her major novels. The *Times Literary Supplement*, for example, ran a full-length article, "A Corvo of Our Day," in which the reviewer concludes that "in lighting out for such new territory . . . she has confected an admirable short tragi-comedy, and again shown herself as interesting a novelist as any in the country."[2] As far as the other two novels, *Night and Silence, Who Is Here? An American Comedy* (1963), and *Cork Street, Next to the Hatter's: A Novel in Bad Taste* (1965), are concerned, the reception has been less enthusiastic. Granville Hicks probably voices the sentiments of many readers when he suggests that *The Unspeakable Skipton* "is much the best, not because it raises any profound moral or literary issue but because Skipton is such a magnificent character.

By comparison the other two are diffuse and a little pallid. They
have their entertaining episodes, but they make no such impression
as Skipton."[3]

It is rather remarkable that the same year should see the publication of both *The Humbler Creation* and *The Unspeakable Skipton*
because they can so easily be seen as opposites. The protagonist of
the first is an essentially virtuous man who sacrifices himself in
order to do his duty to others, whereas the protagonist of the second
is unspeakably selfish and unscrupulous. Walter Allen wonders if
some of the details of Skipton's personality—"that ferocious anal-
eroticism, that passion for cleanliness, that revulsion from the contacts of the flesh"—don't come "very near to a perverted saintliness"
and suggests that the "intransigence of his appalling lunatic self-
regard almost makes him one of the saints of art."[4] By raising this
issue Walter Allen relates *The Unspeakable Skipton* to the two
books discussed in the previous chapter in which the author tenta-
tively explores the question of what makes a person a saint in
modern society and describes two people who are martyrs to their
circumstances. It is easy to suppose that after having made a penetrating analysis of such people the author was tempted to explore
the personality of the kind of person who does not hesitate to exploit
others for his own ends.

Daniel Skipton, the protagonist of *The Unspeakable Skipton*,
has a real-life counterpart in Frederick Rolfe. Johnson acknowledges
the resemblance between her fictional creation and the self-styled
Baron Corvo, and many readers of Alphonse J. A. Symon's biography *The Quest for Corvo* (1955) will recognize one of her
sources.[5] In 1977, Johnson reviewed a recent biography of Frederick
Rolfe for the *Times Literary Supplement* and her description of
him there can almost be used as a brief character sketch of Skipton
(except that Skipton is a voyeur rather than a pederast): "Paranoiac, pederast, pimp and scrounger, biter of hands that fed him;
photographer, ecclesiastic, painter, writer; some talent, not much,
but a streak of pure genius; abnormal physical courage and endurance."[6]

Skipton was born in London but lives in Bruges, where he

scrounges on gullible tourists and pimps to supplement his monthly allowance from "Flabby Anne" and his meager income from reviewing English books for a Belgian paper. The novel describes the last few weeks of his life, showing how he attaches himself to a group of English tourists whom he believes to be easy prey but who see through him and defeat him. As the author of "A Corvo of Our Day" perceptively remarks, much of the substance of the comedy "comes from this Jonsonian situation of the biter bit."[7] Johnson gives it an additional touch of irony by making Skipton's intended victims two self-proclaimed artistic geniuses who are every bit as unspeakable as Skipton and who thoroughly deserve the fate Skipton intends for them.

The dominant member of the group that Skipton picks on is Dorothy Merlin, an overbearing "Australian-born playwright, whose verse dramas had given her a vogue in esoteric circles in London and were inevitably produced in reading editions with long, admiring prefaces by herself" (p. 15). Dotty (as she is appropriately called) is the mother of seven sons and suffers from a most amusing "womb complex." She mouths clichés about motherhood and the Oedipus complex. She is a complete caricature of the phony artist, and Johnson has a great deal of fun at her expense. Dotty is spending a week or ten days in Bruges accompanied by her husband, Cosmo Hines, the owner of a book shop in Cork Street, who has determined to draw the line at the seventh son and is forced to find fulfillment elsewhere. Two friends, Matthew Pryar, an upper-class snob who enjoys dancing "lightly round the fringes of literature,"[8] and Duncan Moss, a good-natured, foolish young photographer who is habitually drunk and in love, are also traveling with Dotty, who spends most of her time calling them to heel.

Skipton introduces himself to the group as "Knight of the Most Noble Order of SS. Cyril and Methodius" with a romantic story about how he acquired it. He is "never sure whether or not to believe it himself, since parts of it were true" (p. 21). He immediately starts to drop hints about the possibility of introducing Cosmo and his friends to the seamier side of life in Bruges and by pretending total disinterest in it himself awakens their curiosity enough to ensure he will trap all of them (including Dotty) into attending his favorite performance of Leda and the Swan. When he finds they do not respond to his efforts to get them to buy a painting from a disreputable antique dealer from whom Skipton gets a commission, he determines to try to dupe an Italian count, Querini, who has joined Dotty's group and get him to buy the picture instead.

Querini is a mirror-image of Skipton. He too has a romantic, aristocratic background and thinks of himself as a great artist—his dream is to give a concert at Wigmore Hall and win public recognition. Although elements in the image he projects are true, it is essentially false and he is nothing less than a confidence-trickster. Ironically enough, he turns the tables on Skipton by pretending to accept his opinion that the disreputable antique dealer is selling a geniune Flemish master at a ridiculously low price. He then borrows money from Skipton "in order to pay for it" and disappears rapidly from the scene. Cosmo Hines also plays a part in tricking Skipton as a revenge for the insults Skipton has heaped on Dorothy in a moment of rage. He is the one who advises Querini to borrow the money from Skipton and then encourages Skipton to lend it, knowing full well that Querini's credentials are dubious. In the end Cosmo pours salt on Skipton's wounds by writing him a polite letter explaining what he has done and why.

The story ends with a picture of Skipton left to die—deserted by Dorothy and her group, tricked by Querini, rejected by his publisher, and cut off by "Flabby Anne." Even Mimi, who owed him a commission for bringing Cosmo to her brothel, does him out of it by falling down the steps and breaking her neck! Yet with his fortunes at their nadir Skipton remains convinced of his own genius and the imbecility of the world around him and by a strange paradox his spirit emerges triumphant.

In a prefatory note Johnson states that she "always wanted to write a study of an artist's paranoia" (p. vii). But in Skipton she creates much more than a paranoiac artist—she also explores the artist's megalomania and feelings of misanthropy toward the inferior beings who remain blind to his genius. Even though Skipton has written only one decadent historical novel, *The Damask and the*

Blood, he is convinced that the work he is engaged on will someday
be a universally acclaimed masterpiece. The lines that he polishes
so assiduously, however, reveal less of his genius than of his vene-
mous hatred of the people with whom he deals, even those who are
undoubtedly trying to help him. The much-abused publisher, Ut-
terson, is not as "unutterable" as Skipton feels he is, and his cousin,
"Flabby Anne," is less rich and more generous than he is willing
to believe.

Throughout the novel Johnson relates episodes chronologically
entirely from Skipton's point of view. This technique has the effect
of making the reader sympathize with him in spite of his moral
reprehensibility. Since he is a writer, Skipton has an extraordinary
gift for words and his venom is often singularly amusing. The scene
where he can no longer hide the contempt he feels for "Dorothy
Merlin, half-witted lyre-bird, pretentious rudas," is superbly comic
(p. 217).

Skipton's feelings are often reflected in the way that he sees his
surroundings. Directly after he has snubbed Dorothy he exits "with
the lovely bells dancing all about him and *Maritana* crashing away
from the bandstand like the triumphant chorus of all the heavenly
hosts at the final banishing of evil from the earth" (p. 217). However, he also remembers the deprivation of the previous winter
when "the iron bells had rung death and starvation in their hundred
coarse voices" (p. 57). Both these examples demonstrate the way
in which the prospect alters according to Skipton's emotional state.
Johnson has used this technique earlier in several of her serious
novels but nowhere does she use it as consistently and as effectively
as she does in this work.

Because Skipton is so fond of Bruges and knows it inside out, the
novel is also full of lyrical descriptions of the city. As one critic
points out, "Bruges fits the unspeakable Skipton like a glove."[9] The
author imbues the entire novel with the sounds, smells, colors, and
atmosphere of Bruges, which she herself loves. Roger Becket feels
that "the best pages in the book are the Flemish landscapes, which
are neither fiction nor caricature, but intently observed scenes in a
country where the presence of sea level is sovereign, where the

weather can change radically in a few minutes, where the air is full of carillons and the buildings are always reflected in the shimmer of canals."[10]

The characterization of Skipton and the creation of an ideal setting give *The Unspeakable Skipton* a quality that raises it above the level of a simple comedy. There is also an undercurrent of genuine pathos in Skipton's plight. Thus the novel is imbued with that "finest sort of humour" which, according to Bernard Shaw, "draws a tear along with the laugh."[11]

Night and Silence, Who Is Here? An American Comedy

The second novel in the series suffers by comparison with *Skipton*, although it is a skillfully written satire of the academic world. Perhaps the author intends to establish an ironic contrast between the two books with the situation of genius starving in a garret in one and pseudoscholarship thriving in a rich New England college in the other.

Matthew Pryar, the protagonist of *Night and Silence, Who Is Here?*, finds himself elevated to the position of a world authority on Dorothy Merlin simply because he has written a couple of articles on her work. Cobb, a richly endowed college in New Hampshire, obligingly invites him to spend a term there as a visiting fellow in order to write a book on her. Soon after his arrival and a few abortive efforts to apply himself to the task, Matthew realizes that he has no gift for literary research but convinces himself that his real gifts are those of an administrator instead. No sooner has he formulated the desire to become director of the center than Dr. Parke announces his decision to retire from the post. The wheels of intrigue are set in motion as Matthew tries to get himself appointed Dr. Parke's successor. He uses the well-tried tricks of the academic politician—dropping a word in the ear of one of his friends who is a trustee and enlisting the help of Jane Merle, a powerful American multimillionairess who uses her telephone with remarkable effect. Just when he seems within reach of his goal, Matthew's hopes are completely dashed. J. L. Walters, a deceptively unimpressive-look-

ing man whom Matthew dislikes, turns out to be the most influential of all the trustees and refuses to vote for Matthew because he
insisted on being repaid for a small loan he had made J. L. Moreover, Dr. Parke, who was well on the way to proposing Matthew,
changes his mind when he gets pushed down the stairs and suspects
Matthew of having done the deed. As a final blow, Dorothy Merlin
arrives on the campus in order to take Matthew to task for having
failed to produce the book she is so eager to have him publish. Then
Jane Merle arrives like a *deus ex machina* and rescues Matthew by
offering to marry him and keep him in luxury for the rest of his
life—an offer he is too wise to refuse.

Many readers who know C. P. Snow's novel *The Masters* (1937)
will readily see that Johnson has written a comic version of her
husband's novel about the politics of academic power. As *Time's*
reviewer remarks, "it looks like a Snow family specialty."[12] However, the author herself seems to have had Shakespeare's *Midsum-
mer Night's Dream* in mind, and points the reference by quoting
the appropriate lines from Puck's speech on the title page. Indeed
the woods of the New Hampshire college can be compared to the
grove near Athens and the same kind of absurd antics take place
in them. Matthew and Jane Merle can be seen as a reversal of the
roles of Oberon and Titania, with Matthew as the bemused fairy
who is attracted to the idea of writing about the freakish monster
Dorothy Merlin, and dreams of becoming King of Cobb. Then his
beloved queen wakes him to a fairy-tale "reality" and the two of
them wander off to live happily ever after. There is no doubt that
Puck is the author of the fantasy.

The story offers Johnson ample opportunity to poke fun at many
aspects of both British and American life. Matthew is the complete
English gentleman, an inveterate snob who has not done a stroke
of work since he came down from Oxford. Jane is the stereotype of
the rich American widow, with an infinite trust in the capacity of
her bank account to arrange everything to her satisfaction.

All the scholars at Cobb College are a bunch of grotesques who
would feel at home in a Dickens novel. There is Dr. Maud Groby,
the drunken Slavonic specialist; Dr. Hefflinger, the fanatical aran-

eologist who carries poisonous spiders about his person and speaks
lovingly of them as man's best friends. Then there is Dr. Edith
Corall, who faints at the sight of a spider, thinks lovingly of Cambridge (England), and looks lost without her bicycle. The most
amusing of them all is Dr. Ruddock, who is single-minded in his
search for lines in Emily Dickinson's poetry that will prove his
hypothesis that she was an alcoholic. These and several other cari-
catures give the novel a farcical tone that is very different from the
rest of Pamela Hansford Johnson's fiction.

There are also several exaggerated episodes that satirize academic
life. One of the most amusing is the one in which Matthew allows
himself to be blackmailed by the unsocial sociologist, Dr. Tiepolo,
in the hope of escaping from the duty of giving a public lecture.
When he loses his money but still has to lecture he is seized by
panic and then unexpectedly saved by Dr. Edith Corall. An expert
medievalist, she can lecture on any subject "from Beowulf to cyber-
netics," and she advises Matthew to plead laryngitis while she takes
over and revenges herself on Dorothy for having criticized her dress
at a party in Oxford some years ago.[13]

While the novel is replete with such nonsensical situations there
are a few moments when the author introduces a philosophic reflection that is reminiscent of her comments in the serious novels.
Thus when Dr. Wohlgemutt tells Matthew how wrong it was of
him to criticize Dr. Parke because the poor man is beset with personal problems the author comments: "There are few things more
disturbing than to find, in somebody we detest, a moral quality
which seems demonstrably superior to anything we ourselves possess. . . . We demand that people should be true to the pictures we
have of them, no matter how repulsive those pictures may be: we
prefer the true portrait (as we have conceived it), in all its homoge-
neity, to one with a detail added which refuses to fit in. Sainthood
is acceptable only in saints" (p. 174). In spite of its comic context
there is more than a grain of truth in this observation.

As a rule, however, the author's voice serves to underline the
satire in this novel, as when she observes of Matthew that "there
had been three cardinal sins in the eyes of his family, lying, eaves-

dropping and being rude to servants. The first sin he had of course, learned to commit fairly frequently in a white and modest fashion— a man must grow up. But he had not yet committed the other two" (pp. 216–17). The tongue-in-cheek endorsement of these false values makes the satire more complex than it appears to be on the surface. A similar effect is gained when she describes Matthew's feelings as he enters an American roadside bar

which, in its orange and peacock whimsy, its impeccable cleanliness, seemed to him suddenly like the desire-image of the whole human race. If the world did not blow up, it would with the centuries be covered all over with places such as these, planted in the deserts, the jungles the swamps reclaimed: french fries for all, and a pretty wonderful thing too. Already all over America these pretty Disneyesque buildings proliferated, offering nowhere a disappointment: for everything you were offered, any old place, would be precisely the same, not even a variation in the thickness of a hamburger. (p. 242)

Here the author's comment has the effect of making the reader reject the prospect of a world full of such places while ostensibly praising them. The casual reference to the threat of a nuclear explosion that hangs over contemporary man makes it doubly ironic that the alternative to such a fate should be the uniformity of an American snack bar. If the writer had used such comments as a consistent way of viewing the world she has created in this novel, it would have gained considerably in meaning. Unfortunately, however, she is content to strew these gems at random and the dominant impression that the book leaves is one of rollicking fun without the depth that a more trenchant treatment of the subject could have achieved.

Cork Street, Next to the Hatter's: A Novel in Bad Taste

The vein of serious comment is more pronounced in the third novel in the trilogy, where Pamela Hansford Johnson is deeply concerned about her subject. Thus, for example, she expresses disapproval of the way in which art has run into an experimental cul-de-sac in many of her critical articles. She also feels that the trend among contemporary writers to include violence and crime in their work can have a deleterious effect on susceptible minds and asks for a more responsible society in her study *On Iniquity* (1967).[14] Although this book was published two years later than *Cork Street* the novel conveys a similar message, even though it is presented comically.

Tom Hariot, a university lecturer in structural linguistics, pleads for sounder moral values in literature. He does this by deciding "to write a play so nauseating that it could not, in any circumstances be allowed on any stage" (p. 23). Even though he succeeds in putting every imaginable indecency into *The Potted Shrimp* he finds that there are people who are so blinded by literary fashion that they are willing to hail it as a masterpiece. Tom is alarmed when an avant-garde director decides to stage the play but continues to cherish the fond belief that good sense will prevail—until it is too late. On the first night he stands up to denounce the play and creates such a stir that he defeats his own purpose—the critics find it impossible to judge the play. Sick with despair Tom decides "it had all gone for nothing. He had caused his detestable play to be ignored, he had not made his point at all, and he had lost his job" (p. 234). At this point Jane arrives and lives up to her earlier role as a fairy godmother. She promises to find something for Tom to do in America: "Teaching your queer subject, or perhaps dramaturgy —what do you think? I might even manage a full professorship if I gave some new institution a new dormitory. or [sic] library, or psychiatric centre. That is for the authority concerned to decide. You might go to Cobb College, in New Hampshire—yes, why not? I believe it is quite pleasant now, not difficult, as it was in poor Matt-Matt's day" (p. 240). Thus Tom can start afresh in America, and the only hope for the return of sanity to British literary life is represented by a young girl whom Tom meets in the street just before the first night of his play. Tom finds that his self-imposed contact with vulgarity and brutality affects his own behavior and is relieved when he meets a girl, Lanti, who is unwilling to countenance bad manners. Harold, his friend, points out that "with every Lanti, . . . there is hope for the world" and tells Tom to "think of her as your salvation, because, from one of these little ones, salvation is going to come" (pp. 222–223).

Although the main story revolves around Tom and his "beastly play" the fact that he is one of Dorothy Merlin's new friends makes it possible for Pamela Hansford Johnson to introduce several of the characters who were with her in Bruges—Cosmo Hines, Duncan Moss, and Matthew Pryar. Dorothy is even more tiresome than she was when parading as an artist in Bruges. Through her the author can satirize all the literary clichés she wishes to expose. Thus Dorothy insists on talking about the "different levels" of art, she fatuously claims that the most dreadful literature is "so true," and she maintains that a writer's intentions have nothing to do with the work he produces. Once Tom has written his play, Dorothy is the first one to proclaim it a masterpiece.

The contrast between the world depicted in the play and Tom's everyday world is clearly established and helps to point to the lesson that life is not as full of violence and crime as modern literature makes it seem. Tom discusses every detail of the play's composition with his friend Harold Boulton in an atmosphere of cozy domesticity which is a perfect foil to the horrible stuff he is concocting. Similarly Jane Pryar goes to visit a prison where she meets a real-life criminal whom she finds exceedingly dull (p. 113). There is also the case of an aspiring young author, Pringle Milton, who is writing a book called *The Cruel Ones* in which she slavishly follows the current trends, but she herself is delightfully innocent and best suited to pose as a cute kitten for Duncan Moss, whose posters of her make her famous, much to her chagrin.

Pringle provides the novel with an amusing subplot. She falls hopelessly in love with Tom and keeps insisting that his play is really very good. Ultimately she makes the gesture of supreme self-sacrifice by publicly supporting Tom when he stands up to condemn his play. There is a brief moment when Jane Pryar is "saddened to the heart" by the prospect of Pringle's unrequited passion but because it is no more than a moment the author succeeds in treating comically a theme that she has treated seriously in other novels.

The relationship between Cosmo and Dorothy is one where the author also makes fun of a situation that she usually treats seriously —an unhappy marriage. Cosmo no longer loves Dorothy: "It was a long time since he had felt impelled to put the finishing touches to the ruin of the writer Skipton simply because Skipton had insulted Dorothy in the high style, the grand manner" (p. 142). There is a revealing scene between Cosmo and Dorothy in which the writer successfully blends a serious view of their marriage with a comic treatment of their incompatibility. Dorothy is trying to force Cosmo to admit he still loves her:

Bold is the man who can say, just simply, "No." Many men are hard enough not to care about the effect of a "no" upon the recipient: but if the recipient happens to be a wife, they had better care (and they usually do) about the result of a "No" upon themselves. For life has to be trundled through somehow, when two people dislike each other but are too weary, or too afraid, to go through the grimy hodgepodge of separation or divorce. Cosmo said, "No." (pp. 142–43)

The truth behind this reflection and the deflatory effect of the brief statement, "Cosmo said, 'No,'" creates an ambivalent effect. A similar blend of the comic with the serious is produced at the end when, without preparing the reader beyond the introductory chapter in which Dorothy visits the doctor, it proves that Dorothy is suffering from a fatal disease. The news is conveyed in vague terms by the doctor who telephones Cosmo, whose reaction is to light a cigar "by way of a treat for himself" (p. 248).

It is in fact characteristic of this novel that the writer combines absurdity with seriousness. She seems to have deliberately adopted the traditional stance of the eighteenth-century satirist, who kept an ironic distance from his subject, while holding up a mirror to society in the hope of making it see its own failings. This may be the reason for her adoption of the chapter headings characteristic of Fielding's novels, such as "The reader herewith is made acquainted with a bookshop, a photographer, and with a young woman of peculiar countenance" (p. 6). It is interesting to note that her own subtitle is "a novel in bad taste" and to enquire if she is ironically suggesting that her novel is in bad taste because it is dealing with an unfashionable subject.[15] Granville Hicks feels she has confused literary and moral issues: "If a play should not be regarded as good just because it is dirty, neither is dirtiness a reason for calling it bad."[16] This is a return to the age-old issue of the relationship between art and morality, and here Johnson is unfashionable enough to suggest that the moral quality of a work is related to its literary value as well.

Thus, although each one of the books is primarily comic in intention, deeper analysis reveals an underlying seriousness and concern with social problems that is characteristic of the author. Pamela Hansford Johnson admits that she has a special affection for the Dorothy Merlin Comedies.[17] Even though only *The Unspeakable Skipton* can be ranked with her best work, the others bring to the surface the qualities of wit and humor which are almost always present even in her most serious work.

Chapter Ten

Human Relationships and Moral Values

Four of Pamela Hansford Johnson's novels remain to be considered: *An Error of Judgement* (1962), *The Honours Board* (1970), *The Good Listener,* (1975) and *The Good Husband* (1978). Whereas the latter two easily form a unit with the same protagonist and several characters in common, the first two cannot easily be forced into a common mold. Since all four can be dealt with in a single chapter it seems most convenient to deal with them in chronological order. All four novels do share a quality which can be said to be one of the distinguishing characteristics of Pamela Hansford Johnson's fiction: an interest in human relationships and the moral values by which people live. Although this is a quality which is to be found in several of the novels already discussed and cannot be said to be the special province of these four novels, it seems appropriate in this final chapter to focus on a subject that has been one of the novelist's major concerns.

An Error of Judgement

The two novels that preceded *An Error of Judgement* (*The Humbler Creation* and *The Unspeakable Skipton*) throw some light on the development of the author's interest in the problem of distinguishing good from evil, the saint from the sinner. Maurice Fisher is conceived of as the good man who believes in self-sacrifice and doing his duty. Skipton is at the other extreme, a selfish scavenger who does not hesitate to exploit people. William Setter, the central character in *An Error of Judgement,* can be thought of as either a saint or as a sinner depending upon the moral premises of the person who judges him. The novel shows how difficult it is to judge such a man and implies that either judgment would be erroneous.

In trying to present Setter's moral dilemma, Pamela Hansford Johnson adopts a rather complex narrative technique. Setter's story is told by Victor Hendrey, a man whose life is considerably affected by Setter when their paths cross. He is endowed with an unusual degree of self-irony and humor so that he can distance himself not only from his friend, whom he does not fully understand, but also from his own experience. A further sense of distance is created by inserting the stories of three different characters within the framework of Victor's account and labeling them quite simply, "Setter's Story," "Sammy's Story," and "Emily's Story." These specially defined episodes focus on Setter's inner moral dilemma, whereas the framework in which they are placed concentrates on the more mundane plane of outer action.

The narrator, a man with a tendency toward hypochondria, first meets William Setter, a Harley Street physician, when he consults him for cardiac disease. Setter makes a profound impression upon him and Victor leaves his rooms feeling miraculously well. Not long afterwards, he meets Setter again in the most bizarre circumstances at a party in New York and finds the roles are reversed. This time Setter is in trouble and needs a shoulder to cry on. Once back in London, Victor, his wife, Jenny, and his troublesome mother-in-law, Stephanie, are all drawn into Setter's circle. Setter's wife, Emily, a beautiful American blonde, is no longer in love with her husband and excels in having "platonic lovers." When Setter learns, somewhat painfully, that her latest love is far from platonic he is completely disillusioned and gives up his career. Once Emily realizes that the knighthood she has been waiting for is permanently out of her reach, she leaves Setter and marries her lover.

At the same time that Setter's marriage breaks up, Victor finds his own marriage is threatened. His wife is plunged into grief when her mother dies on the only occasion that Jenny insists upon leaving her with one of her sisters so that she can accept the Setters' invitation to their home. Victor adds to Jenny's grief by telling her not to feel guilty, thereby ensuring that she will. Jenny begins to have nightmares in which she dreams of her mother rising out of hell to drag her down into the bottomless pit and turns to Setter for help. Before long, Victor realizes that Jenny is in love with Setter but can do very little to alter the situation. Eventually Jenny tells Setter of her love. His rejection of her releases her and she persuades herself that she is in love with Victor once more.

This somewhat conventional drama of human relationships is the framework within which is set the story of Setter's personal moral dilemma. An early experience has convinced Setter that he is born evil and derives pleasure from inflicting pain. Although he does not believe in God he is aware of being constantly watched and feels damned. The irony of his life seems to be that he feels compelled to struggle to be good even though he knows he cannot change his own evil nature. Setter is tested when he becomes involved with the case of Sammy Underwood, a juvenile delinquent who has committed a brutal murder. The narrator also acts as the link between Setter and Sammy since Malpass, the priest who is interested in finding out whether or not Sammy is responsible for murder, is one of Victor's oldest friends. Sammy starts attending Setter's weekly meetings for his problem patients and becomes dependent on Setter. Setter uses this dependency to force a confession from Sammy. Once he is convinced that Sammy has killed and will kill again he takes it upon himself to put him out of the way. The important thing is that he finds he derives no pleasure from carrying out his decision. If, as Setter himself suggests, God would be making an error of judgment were he to consider him good simply because he has never done anything evil without looking into his heart, then by implication it would also be an error of judgment to condemn him when he murders with good intent. This is the hypothesis the novel explores.

Setter's action in killing Sammy is further complicated by relating it to "the state of the world." At the beginning of the book Malpass, Victor, and Jenny discuss the threat of nuclear war. The priest says, "I can never escape the feeling that all statesmen are mad. Being mad is a prerequisite for the job. What can 'losing face' matter, metaphorically, if the alternative is losing it in a perfectly literal sense?"[1] Throughout the novel there are reminders that the world seems bent on destroying itself, and at the end of the book Malpass connects Sammy's death with world affairs: "Well, it was no nine days wonder, not for the world at large, seriously and madly contemplating burning itself to ashes." Victor then recalls the words of their first conversation: "Were people so crazy? Statesmen so crazy? But then, it was a question of *Losing Face*. Damn funny, when the alternative was no face to lose—Had somebody said that before? Conceivably, one had to think of individual faces to keep sane" (p. 216). The fact that Victor emphasizes the importance of the individual suggests that the case of Sammy and Setter should be related to the way men murder each other during war. Setter is also linked to the prevailing fear of a holocaust when Victor meets a physicist in Cambridge who reminds him of Setter. He learns that the physicist has given up his work with atomic energy in order to devote himself to health physics instead, and immediately links Setter's behavior with that of this scientist: "I thought of Setter, who had also tried to castrate his own power to do harm, and was finding it difficult. But Setter was not a sure man, not as this man was. And his enemy was not the tools of harm, but the harm he fancied within himself, built into his own being, as much part of the total structure as rib-cage or spinal column" (p. 183). Because of the emphasis on world affairs the reader looks for a connection between them and Setter's story. Yet Setter's struggle with his sense of sin has very little logical relation to the affairs of the world even though the writer obviously intends some such relationship to emerge.

In addition to suggesting that Setter can be regarded as a saint or a madman there are several references in the text that link him with a dog. His very name suggests a hunting dog and it is therefore rather ironic that his pejorative term for psychologists, whom he mistrusts, is "dog-face" (pp. 3, 24). The irony becomes even more pronounced when Setter gives up his medical practice and starts to run a club for "lame dogs," where his role is very similar to that of a psychologist. Jenny states this quite plainly when she tells her husband, " 'He means nothing to me, except as a doctor.' She pulled away smiling at me wanly. 'Well, a dog-face' " (p. 142). Toward the end of the book Setter admits that, in spite of his efforts to avoid being a psychologist, many of his patients have treated him as one: "I'm not a dog-face. . . . I should have been a rotten one. I never tried to be one at all. But I may have done harm when people didn't understand" (p. 199). Sammy also connects Setter with a dog when he comes to see him in his rooms. Shocked by the scruffiness of Setter's surroundings, he tells him that he wouldn't even let his dog live in such a state. All these scattered references encourage the reader to attach special significance to Setter's name and to see him as a kind of hunting dog who tracks down the victim. But instead of waiting, as the well-trained setter should, for the hunter to come and cast his net over both the dog and the prey, he takes it upon himself to act and kills. Does this mean he has done wrong? It is impossible to judge.

While Setter is an extraordinary man, Victor Hendrey, through whose eyes he is shown, is quite recognizably a type out of Pamela Hansford Johnson's earlier fiction. He lives a "couple of tube stations away from Clapham," he has marched in the 1930s, and he has settled down into comfortable bourgeois respectability in the 1950s (p. 70). The "ordinariness" of his life and problems is emphasized. "We live, and we talk, as if we expected our world of squares to go on for ever" (p. 70). It is difficult to decide whether or not there is a criticism of Victor's limited horizons implicit in the description of his life. On the one hand, he and Jenny do not have any children, which suggests a barren relationship, and at the end of the book when Jenny promises him that she is in love with him he says, "Of course, I didn't believe a word of it, because I do not think that love, once destroyed, ever returns" (p. 251). On the other hand, he feels "glad for us both that Jenny meant what she had said, because if she went on believing she was in love with me it would be almost as good as if she really were so. . . . Really good acting becomes a kind of truth" (p. 252). The ability to compromise reflected in this statement is shown to be a much more durable quality than Setter's moral stringency. Setter loses his wife, his son, his job; he commits murder and in the end he simply disappears. Victor and Jenny, on the other hand, go on cultivating their garden: "The garden-soil seems to be getting richer. Jenny is thinking of planting begonias next year. I tell her it will look far too like the factory, not a home from home but a work from works; she pays no attention. I suppose, after a time, I shan't notice them; after all, there are other things than begonias in life" (p. 252). As a concluding paragraph this is remarkably ambivalent. The tidy squares and the garden like a factory sound too provincial and circumscribed altogether, but there is an element of wisdom in Victor's resigned comment that "there are other things than begonias in life." It also implies there was truth in Victor's contention, earlier in the novel, that "if there is any health in the world, I think a bit of it is with us" (p. 70). Martin Price confirms Victor's judgment. He feels that the narrator "is perhaps the finest creation in the book. In contrast with Setter, he is a man who has wryly come to terms with himself. . . . As opposed to Setter, he seems to be offered as an alternative version—unheroic and yet somewhat admirable—of the much-discussed liberal imagination."[2] The author's voice does not intrude, and the reader is left to make up his own mind whether Victor is meant to be an unheroic hero or a philistine.

An Error of Judgement is in many ways one of the most ambitious novels Pamela Hansford Johnson has written. It contains several elements that she has shown her ability to deal with skillfully in her earlier fiction. Victor's life, especially his relationship with his mother-in-law, Stephanie, whom he has liked and found good fun, but who becomes difficult and demanding as illness and old age set in, is the kind of life that the author excels at describing. Jenny's grief at her mother's death, her nightmares, and her love for Setter are also well within the author's usual range. Her concern with politics and world affairs is one that is present in many of her novels, for she frequently relates the lives of individuals to a wider background. What is new in this novel, however, is her concern with metaphysical problems.

Although Johnson can only be admired for this effort to extend her range there is a feeling that she is not completely successful. Gerald Sykes of the *New York Times Book Review* is among the most critical:

Miss Johnson has chosen to study an irrelevant kind of evil. Setter possesses no general or symbolic significance; he is an unappealing crank who raises expectations he does not fulfill. Excessive preoccupation with one's own sinfulness does exist, and the Calvinist mentality is far from departed from the modern world; but as treated here, it seems more like a personal obsession of the author's than an analyzable force that we can study with profit or enjoy esthetically.[3]

It is not really necessary for Setter's case to possess "general or symbolic significance" but unfortunately the author herself seems to imply it does through the many references to evil in society. Even more troubling than this is the fact that the novel seems to gather together so many different ideas without weaving them into a discernible pattern. Thus, for example, the detailed descriptions of Jenny's vision of hell and the reiteration of the information that neither Emily nor Sammy can dream seems to be very significant. Yet these details shed no apparent light on Setter's fear of damnation, nor do they link up with the central theme. Similarly, if Setter is meant to be a man who destroys, in spite of himself, the people with whom he comes into contact, then what significance should be attached to the way he helps two of his "lame dogs"—Lawson, a manly woman with a yearning for love and protection, and Purdue, a weak man who does not get on with anybody—to find each other and marry? Even when it comes to the essential contrast between Setter and Victor the fact that the author establishes it but does not work it out leaves a sense of frustration. It is one of the few cases where the reader wishes that the novelist had provided some indication of how to interpret her theme. If the whole point is simply to show that some men are larger than life, live at a greater pitch of moral intensity, and are destined to work out their fate no matter what the cost, whereas some men compromise and carry on living, then the complexity of the novel hardly seems justified. This may be true to life, but art should impose a pattern upon life. This is why, in the last analysis, *An Error of Judgement* is not artistically satisfying, even though it compels recognition of the author's effort to try to deal with a subject that only the most serious novelists would consider treating in fiction.

The Honours Board

The Honours Board (1970) is a return to the type of fiction that Pamela Hansford Johnson has already mastered. The story, told in the third person, is set in a young boy's boarding school, where she can make use of a closed community to gather together several people and expose their individual problems. Downs Park is an image of a wider world where values are changing and the old order yielding place to new. The headmaster, Cyril Annick, looks across his school and asks himself, "How much longer could these schools exist economically, or be regarded still as social and academic necessities?"[4] The end of the book suggests that some important values will disappear when they do. The school is taken over by the Massingers, the two members of his staff whom he most dislikes and who are radically opposed to everything Cyril and his wife, Grace, represent. Cyril has struggled to keep the fees low, avoided corporal punishment, encouraged the science side, and dreamt of getting at least one brilliant pupil. Rupert Massinger is determined to make the school a paying proposition; believes firmly in discipine; intends to get rid of the gifted science master, whom he can't abide; and dreams of carving a name for the school in sports activities. The struggle between these two is symbolized by the beautiful thicket in the school grounds which the boys use as a refuge from prying eyes. Cyril loves the thicket, but the first thing that Rupert intends to do is to cut it down. However, before he leaves the school, Cyril realizes his most cherished wish. Peter Quillan, the gifted student whom he admitted at the beginning of the book, and with whom he establishes a very special relationship, succeeds in topping the list of the applicants for Eton and has his name printed in golden letters on the school's honors board. The novel clearly shows that the values that Cyril and Grace have stood for are more humane and the passing of them is profoundly to be regretted. Grace's death, soon after her husband has sold the school, plunges Cyril into grief and can be seen as a symbol for the passing away of a civilized world.

Although the power struggle between the Annicks and the Massingers represents the moral core of the novel, there are a great many other threads to the narrative. The staff at Downs Park are a fair cross-section of humanity. Rupert Massinger, the games master, is the embodiment of virility and finds it impossible to be faithful to his wife, Blossom. He makes love to his secretary, Helen Queen, and Blossom is most upset when she discovers that all her efforts to match her husband's desires have been in vain. Gradually, however, she learns to ignore his infidelities and support him in all his ventures.

Penelope, the Annicks' widowed daughter, is a restless young woman who gives in to sexual desire and becomes Rupert's mistress. She is afraid to commit herself to the science master, Leo Canning, even though he is deeply in love with her. Leo has a lower-class background which troubles Penelope. He also has old-fashioned ideas on sex and marriage. Consequently it takes Penelope a long time to accept his proposal. The growth of the relationship between them is very convincingly traced and is an excellent example of the author's skill at penetrating the human heart.

Like most closed communities, Downs Park has its share of unhappy and lonely individuals. Betty Cope, the undermatron, is a lesbian whose friend, Gwen Morphy, makes her suffer all the agonies of a one-sided love affair. She, in turn, becomes the center of the starved affections of the elderly French teacher, Mrs. Murray. Mrs. Murray's passion is truly tragic. The emotional strain she suffers drives her to kleptomania. In order to convey her suffering Pamela Hansford Johnson enters into her mind the way she did in several of her earlier psychological novels. Mrs. Murray feels compelled to steal by a force outside herself, and the school is greatly disturbed when things begin to disappear. Eventually Helen Queen, who has a talent for snooping, catches Mrs. Murray red-handed and helps her to return whatever she has stolen. Even though Helen will never reveal her identity, Mrs. Murray is unable to recover from her sense of shame and fears that Betty will find out. Finally she commits suicide by first taking a few sleeping tablets and then drowning herself in the swimming pool.

In addition to a lesbian and a kleptomaniac, the school has the misfortune of employing a new teacher, Norman Poole, whose wife, Delia, is an alcoholic. It doesn't take long for the secret to become common knowledge, and in the end Cyril has no alternative but to accept Norman's resignation.

The Honours Board is an unusual school story in that it focuses upon the lives of the staff rather than upon those of the students. At the same time it succeeds in conveying the impression of a school where the students are a vital part of it. This is done primarily by tracing the relationship between Cyril and his star pupil, Peter, in some detail, and by providing portraits of Peter's friends, rather typical English schoolboys who get up to most of the tricks associated with boarding-school life. The standard events of the school year—Parent's Day, staff parties, the school play, lessons, games, punishments—are all described in a way that makes the school setting entirely credible and three-dimensional. There are also several very beautiful descriptions of nature—of the passing of seasons as the school year progresses, of sunsets as the Annicks' fortunes decline.

A sense of a sound moral perspective on most events is supplied through Grace's observations, for she is endowed with the kind of wisdom that commands respect. One of the questions she asks is clearly related to a question raised by the narrator of *An Error of Judgement*: "I wonder if we can judge by any criterion but individual suffering? . . . Corporate pain? Revolt against parents, against institutions, bad housing. Homes crammed with illegitimate children. Have any of them got names? I find I can only think of the individual person, the single sufferer" (p. 123). This reflection is similar to Victor's observation that "one had to think of individual faces to keep sane." Thus Grace supplies the kind of moral perspective that reveals some of the author's deeper concerns. In this novel, however, such reflections are isolated from each other and do not amount to any consistent "view of life." Nevertheless, the novel has won high praise. William Trevor, for example, feels that "the rich mixture is richly handled, and every development is credible. Miss Hansford Johnson shows again that she is the most professional, most delicate and cleverest of novelists. The pathos in this book is beautifully conveyed, as is the irony, the sense of lives wasted and failing and yet being happy enough, and of lives being wholly miserable."[5] It is indeed true that the author has created a wholly convincing world. Apparently she has deliberately limited her aims, and there is a great deal to be said for this type of fiction as well. As John Knowles points out in his review, "this kind of novel, with its author's implicit claims to omniscience about her characters, its conventional structure and attention to nuance, has a shrinking place in literary fashion today. But I suspect it will prove very durable too."[6]

The Good Listener

In her two most recent novels, *The Good Listener* (1975) and *The Good Husband* (1978), Johnson seems to have set herself the task of creating a contemporary *Comédie humaine*. Her Rastignac is a young man named Toby Roberts who starts life as a student of humble origins and uses women as a means of climbing up the social ladder. At the end of *The Good Listener* the parallel between Toby and Balzac's rogue is made explicit:

There was all London lying below him, and it seemed to him that it was there for the taking.

He did not say, as Rastignac did when surveying Paris from the heights, "It's between the two of us from now on," since Toby had never read a word of Balzac.

But the challenge was there, and he did think something precious like it.[7]

Again in *The Good Husband* the same parallel is drawn: "He felt (though he did not know it) like the young Rastignac starting on the conquest of Paris."[8]

The plot of *The Good Listener* is a simple one. Toby's mother and father, people who run a newsagent's shop in Southeast London, have sacrificed a great deal to send their son to Cambridge. Toby has not been there long before he begins to feel ashamed of his origins: "He could not help it—every time he returned to SE1 he felt like Fanny Price paying a family visit after a long spell at Mansfield Park" (p. 9). When Maisie Ferrars shows signs of falling in love with him, Toby is very much on his guard at the same time that he is eager to exploit her acquaintance. He longs to be invited to Maisie's home, Haddeson, where her widowed mother gives lavish parties for literary people and artists. With a view to obtaining an invitation, Toby invites Maisie to his own home and his parents take to her at once. Toby's mother has considerable artistic ability and her pictures impress Maisie enough to make her arrange an exhibition for Mrs. Roberts at a gallery in Cambridge. This exhibition launches Mrs. Roberts on a modestly successful career and endears Maisie to her for life. Toby also gains his purpose, for he becomes a welcome guest at Haddeson and, in time, begins to sleep with Maisie. Soon even brighter prospects open up for Toby. Claire Falls, the daughter of an earl, meets Toby at one of Mrs. Ferrar's parties and invites him to Glemsford. Toby begins to deceive Maisie, and one of her well-wishers, a perceptive dramatist named Edward Crane, asks Toby not to tamper with her feelings. Still that is exactly what Toby does, and once Maisie realizes Toby has no intention of entering into a permanent relationship with her she tries to commit suicide. Edward saves her and tells Toby, but Toby selfishly persists in his pursuit of Claire. Her family seems willing to accept him and her father helps him to obtain a promising position in a merchant bank. After a great deal of dilly-dallying, Toby comes to the point, only to find that Claire no longer wishes to marry him. Not one to grieve for long, Toby decides he would rather have Maisie after all, but finds she is also out of reach. Edward has asked her to marry him, and Toby is left alone.

Toby's singularly selfish "rake's progress" is contrasted with the destiny of his two closest friends. Bob Cuthbertson, a brilliant physicist, marries a girl he does not love because he has made her pregnant. Bob's marriage is a disaster, but he adores his little daughter and matures through his painful experiences. Adrian Stedman, a man who belongs by birth to the society Toby longs to enter, is a student of theology who intends to become a celibate priest. Both these young men possess a strength of character that Toby noticeably lacks.

Toby's mother is also a complete contrast to her son. Although she achieves worldly success she remains true to her modest origins and refuses to move to finer surroundings. The first time Toby brings Maisie home, he asks his mother to serve cucumber sandwiches and tea because he thinks the homely high-teas she serves in the kitchen reveal his class too well. Mrs. Roberts buys a new tea-trolley and cake-stand and serves tea in the parlor in Maisie's honor, but when Toby brings Claire home for the first time she demonstrates her loyalty to Maisie by refusing to do the same for Claire: "He found that his mother had taken a curious way of getting her own back on him for her distress over Maisie. There were no cucumber sandwiches. There was a marvellous high tea, planned with all her skill, and it was laid in the kitchen" (pp. 173–74). Another symbol of Mrs. Roberts's emotional integrity is the picture she paints of Maisie: "It was a painting of a golden-haired girl in a meadow, less the representation of a girl than of a smile, and it was a smile that Toby knew" (p. 175). When Maisie becomes engaged to Edward, Toby's mother decides to send her the painting as a wedding present: "His mother, an artist in one thing, could not but help to be something of an artist in many others. It would be her way of saying good-bye to Maisie as to someone she could have loved" (p. 235). The truthfulness that is evident in this action is typical of Toby's mother.

Claire and Maisie are skillfully contrasted with each other. The first time Claire meets Toby at a party in Maisie's home, she comes "across the lawn, her boots hard on the daisies" (p. 76). Claire's ruthless pursuit of Toby and the way that she tramples on Maisie is foreshadowed in this brief statement. The author also uses the weather to reflect the difference between the two women. Maisie is associated with sunshine and flowers: "The buds were just greening on the trees, a sooty, bloomy green. There were dwarf daffodils along the margin of the stream. It was unseasonably mild and the sky was a pale blue, washed over by a silvering of sun. The sort of weather appropriate for Maisie; it should be her inner weather always" (p. 128). Claire, on the other hand, is associated with autumn: "The night was sharp, and for him it has still the smell of chrysanthemums. Such weather would henceforth be for him Claire's weather" (p. 151). There are many other differences as well. Maisie is a virgin, and when she comes to Toby's room she offers herself in love. Once he has taken her Toby is "scared of what he had done. Maisie was far removed from the casual girls whom he had taken from time to time, merely for his own easing" (p. 83). The first time Claire and Toby make love is in sharp contrast to this. She suggests it casually, as something they can do quickly before her father comes home, the very first time he visits her, and "unlike Maisie, she was far from inexperienced" (p. 149.) The two women also influence Toby's career in markedly different ways. During his friendship with Maisie, Toby plans to write a thesis on *Saint-Just*, whereas when he turns to Claire he decides to work in a bank. The use of these contrasts helps the author to make it clear that Toby is incapable of appreciating what Maisie offers him and that he makes the wrong choice when he rejects her for Claire.

In this novel every detail has a place in the total conception in a way that shows the author is completely in control of her medium. The meals that are eaten in the different homes are extremely revealing—homemade pork pie and tinned salmon, "which Toby preferred to fresh and always would," in Mrs. Roberts's kitchen; "whitebait, *crepes de volaille*, a *soufflé Grand Marnier*" in Mrs. Ferrar's elegant dining room; dry birds and half-cold bread sauce, or sandwiches hastily prepared and served on a tray in Claire's Tudor mansion. In terms of nourishment (both physical and spiritual) Claire has the least to offer. Another minor detail that assumes symbolic significance is the green lamp Maisie gives Toby as a gift. When he rejects her he switches off the light, but when he is with Claire he still has the lamp in his room and wonders if it bothers Claire that it should be there. At the end of the novel he goes home and unplugs the lamp Maisie had given him "and thrust it into the back of his wardrobe. It should shine on nobody again" (p. 233). Another example of the use of such details is the umbrella that his mother suggests Toby ought to have: "You're bound to get wet sometimes" (p. 219). But Toby has never had an umbrella except as a child, "when his mother came out to take him by the hand and hold the big umbrella aloft over him" (p. 220). This statement deepens in meaning when, after telling him Maisie is not his for the asking, Edward looks out at the rain and offers to lend Toby an umbrella—an offer which he apparently rejects since he walks the streets in misery, his mackintosh "sodden through and the rain . . . streaming down his face" (p. 232). For once in his life Toby does get wet. The development of the author's skill in using this technique is very noticeable because in several of her earlier novels Johnson has used potentially symbolic details but failed to knit them together with her central theme. In this novel, however, all the various elements enrich her basic design.

Somewhat surprisingly, the reviews of *The Good Listener* in two of the most influential literary journals, the *Times Literary Supplement* and the *New York Times Book Review*, are rather negative. Anne Duchêne feels that Toby is "a flabby, passive, unexuberant Rastignac" and Erica Abeel expresses a similar sense of dissatisfaction when she calls Toby a "dreary successor . . . who would conquer worlds with a yawn."[9] It is true that Toby does not have the vitality of his prototype, but surely it would have been a mistake to endow Toby with vitality and charm when he is obviously meant to stand for emotional sterility? Throughout the novel the fact that Toby knows how to listen is stressed and his ability to listen is a symptom of his fear of commitment. Once Maisie tries very hard to get him to talk to her and his reaction is very significant: "But he had heard the alarm-bell ring in his brain. She was trying to enter his mind, which he had only to a certain extent permitted. He wanted to take her to bed. This would at least delay the evil hour of *talking*" (p. 158). The only time that Toby talks is in the crucial final scene with Edward: "He felt that at last he had done enough listening, he began to talk" (p. 231). But it is too late for him to change, and although his first spasm of grief prompts him to write a letter to Maisie begging her to see him, he is sufficiently recovered the next day to feel that the letter is "demeaning to himself" and he tears it up and flushes it away.

Anne Duchêne wants to know why Toby is so evasive and laments the fact that "Miss Hansford Johnson, who has so often handled pain with mastery, is here quite inexplicit about Toby's inner feelings."[10] Yet if Toby's inner feelings were presented from his own point of view it would be much more difficult to condemn the sterility of the values he stands for. He is a type of the "hollow men" of contemporary society. He thinks of life as a staircase (p. 220) and uses people as rungs on his way to the top. The reader's sympathies belong with Edward and Maisie and people like them who value deep feelings and are willing to commit themselves. The issue that the novel raises is one that is extremely relevant to modern society, where people tend increasingly to pursue material gain and shy away from the demands of human relationships. Although the author refrains from moralistic comments and presents her story with a deceptively light touch there can be little doubt that it contains within it a profound criticism of contemporary life.

The Good Husband

The criticism of society implicit in *The Good Listener* is also present in its sequel, *The Good Husband*. The irony in the author's use of "good" is quite unmistakable in this novel about Toby Roberts's continued advancement. Although Toby marries in this book, he remains essentially uncommited and incapable of real emotional experience.

Toby meets Ann Thorold, a well-endowed and beautiful widow, at a party. The attraction that they both feel for each other at their first meeting grows until each of them confesses to being "half in

love with the other" (p. 70). A brief separation, necessitated by a
business trip to New York, serves as a catalyst and results in Ann's
taking the initiative upon Toby's return to London and suggesting
marriage. At the beginning of their marriage Toby seems to be the
more demanding partner, but as time passes Ann takes over this
role. It is typical of their relationship that whereas Toby's demands
center on sexual satisfaction, Ann becomes emotionally dependent
on Toby. As time passes Toby hankers after Maisie, the girl whose
love he rejected as a youth. Once Maisie's husband, Edward Crane
dies, Toby cannot resist the impulse to reawaken her love. Maisie
is too honest a person to enter into a clandestine *affaire* but Toby's
lack of true fidelity hurts Ann very deeply. She betrays her jealousy
in a fit of rage in a key scene that is beautifully realized. Her
vulnerability is contrasted with Toby's ability to go through most
experiences unscathed. As Maisie observes, "Nothing will ever
break you. You're not made that way" (p. 234), and the story suggests that if only Toby could be "broken" he would gain as a human
being.

Many of the characters from the previous novel reappear in *The
Good Husband*. Claire and her husband, Alec Wallace, pick up the
threads of friendship with Toby as easily as Claire cut off her love
affair with him five years earlier. Bob Cuthbertson has become a
famous scientist, a member of the Royal Society, and continues to
adore his daughter, Estella. In time he finds Carol, who will undoubtedly prove a better wife to him than Rita (who forced him
into a shotgun wedding in *The Good Listener*). Adrian Stedman,
the extraordinarily handsome priest, has acquired a wife and help-
mate, Ruth. Rita's passion for Adrian, suggested in the earlier novel,
culminates in her pursuing him with obsessive persistence in this
one. Toby is drawn into a genuine drama of emotions that is being
played out among Rita, her lover, Len, and Adrian, but he sees it
primarily as a good story on which to dine out. Even when Rita's
lover murders her in a fit of jealous passion, Toby attends his trial
out of curiosity rather than out of any genuine feeling for the
people concerned. This lack of involvement is conveyed by having
most of Ruth and Adrian's story "told" rather than enacted. Either

Toby is being told of the latest developments in the lives of his friends through their letters, or else he is telling others what has been happening when they meet.

Throughout this book, Toby's mother, Mrs. Roberts, acts as a contrast to her son, clinging to the values and the way of life to which she was born with fierce pride. Her death after a stroke is one of the few really painful experiences in Toby's life, but after her funeral he returns to his customary role:

It was perfectly satisfactory, his life, or he would make it so. A well-laid table, a well-cooked meal and a handsome woman to preside over it. What more could a man want? If there were dissatisfactions stirring somewhere in his soul, he was scarcely aware of them, or else thought they were a manifestation of indigestion. Toby always preferred the material to the metaphysical. Now he was going to care for Ann all his days, with no more yearning for the Maisies of this world. As if there were one more Maisie in this world! (p. 253)

The ironic voice heard in the authorial aside—"As if there were one more Maisie in this world!"—and in the comment that Toby "always preferred the material to the metaphysical" is typical of the way in which Pamela Hansford Johnson uses the third person to establish distance between Toby and the reader while suggesting Toby is a man capable of charming women. Except for one (perhaps accidental) transition to Ann's point of view—when Mrs. Roberts objects to Ann "railroading" her into staying for dinner and Ann wonders, "Heaven knows where she had got the word" (p. 60), the entire story is presented objectively with a consistent refusal to enter into the minds of characters other than Toby.

The novel is structured around a series of parties and social engagements. It begins and ends with dinner at Clive Baumann's, a senior colleague of Toby's at the merchant bank where he has made a successful career. In between these two parties Toby talks to the people who make up his sphere in a series of encounters over meals in restaurants and invitations to drink or dine. There is a noticeable use of direct speech with the result that the reader is left to overhear Toby and his friends and to judge their words for himself. This creation of what is essentially a novel of "table-talk" has the effect of driving home the triviality of Toby's existence and highlighting his meetings with his mother and Maisie as a contrast.

The novelist uses food as a way of showing the two worlds Toby inhabits in *The Good Husband* in much the same way as she uses it in *The Good Listener*. There is caviar, which Toby eats "with some suspicion and not too much liking" (p. 9) at the Baumanns'. Then there is home-made rabbit pie, which he inwardly regrets having refused at his father's home (p. 270). It is a telling detail that Toby's wife, Ann, "hated rabbit and hare, and refused to eat either" (p. 270), showing that the sophisticated world to which Ann naturally belongs has little in common with the world of Toby's native SE1.

One of the most significant clues to Toby's character is provided by the nightmare that he has after his mother's death in which she shows him two portraits that she has painted. The one is Maisie, symbolized by a curving smile, and the other is Toby, symbolized by a complete blank.

The skill with which Pamela Hansford Johnson can give a detail special significance is demonstrated by the way in which she makes Toby give Ann only semiprecious stones as gifts. The first time he brings her a gift it is a zircon pendant from America that has not cost him too much. The second time he gives her a turquoise ring that he originally bought to give to Claire when he proposed to her in *The Good Listener*. Toby even comments, "I must buy you diamonds one fine day" (p. 163), but, characteristically, he never does. Again it is significant that Toby's marriage to Ann should prove childless. The fact that Ann is too old to have children (and there are times when Toby hankers after a child) is emphasized by mentioning the children that Claire, her brother "Hairy," Maisie, and Bob have on several occasions.

On the other hand there is the use of a picture that Mrs. Roberts gives Toby of a black cat on a patchwork quilt as a detail of potential significance which does not seem to have a carefully worked out meaning. Toby decides to get his mother a quilt like the one she has painted and Ann takes some pains to find her one in an antique shop. When Mrs. Roberts uses the quilt as a cushion for her cat, Blackie, instead of as a coverlet for her own bed, Ann interprets it as a sign that her mother-in-law does not really accept her. This is indeed true, but toward the end of the novel Mrs. Cassell, the widowed neighbor who has agreed to take care of Toby's father after his mother's death, and who will probably be his next wife, uses the patchwork quilt on the bed instead of allowing the cat to have it. The repeated reminders of the patchwork quilt throughout the novel suggest it must have some kind of symbolic function. Yet it is difficult, without exercising considerable ingenuity, to discover what this meaning could be. This failure to integrate the use of a detail as a symbol with the theme of the book suggests that the novelist is not as fully aware of some of the echoes set up by her text as she is in *The Good Listener*.

In spite of the skill with which the novel is written it does not add much to what has already been expressed, and expressed well, in the earlier novel. None of the characters develops beyond what has been indicated in *The Good Listener* and the underlying theme is the same. This is the only book in which Pamela Hansford Johnson has simply repeated herself. In his review for *New Statesman* William Boyd says, "It's hard to imagine such a redoubtably bland character as Toby providing material for one novel, let alone two."[11] Anne Duchêne in the *Times Literary Supplement* is also critical of *The Good Husband*, observing that "it is all, in sum, a little random, like listening to gossip about people one does not know."[12]

Certain elements in the novel are interesting to the people who do know and recognize character types, situations, and motifs from the rest of Johnson's fiction. Toby, for example, is like a modern version of Claud Pickering with his dream of Cecil, whom he could never possess, and the trials of working out a successful relationship with Ellen in *A Summer to Decide*. Ann's fear of old age, even though it is expressed relatively simply by descriptions of her exercises in her bedroom and Toby's irritation at the array of bottles on her dressing table, is reminiscent of Helena's confrontation with the specter of old age in *An Avenue of Stone*. Rita's crazed passion for Adrian and its association with violence recalls the obsessive passion of Melissa in *The Holiday Friend*. The portrayal of Toby's mother, particularly her death, his grief, and his nightmares, is familiar to Johnson's readers as a powerful situation used in other novels as well. Thus *The Good Husband* forms part of the pattern established by the writer's work as a whole and is interesting for that reason rather than because it extends her range.

Chapter Eleven

Conclusion

Any critic faced with the task of defining the nature of Pamela Hansford Johnson's novels finds that, like many of her characters, it belongs to a class that is extremely difficult to label—too good to belong to the middle range but not good enough to belong among the really great. Yet, if, as Iris Murdoch firmly maintains, "it is the function of the writer to write the best book he knows how to write," there can be little doubt that Pamela Hansford Johnson has more than fulfilled her function as a writer.[1] Throughout her long career as a novelist she has demonstrated the seriousness of her commitment to her art and explored those aspects of life that touch upon the experience of most readers with a great deal of lucidity and humaneness.

Looking back over her production it is possible to see how she began writing with a great deal of interest in social problems and the interaction that takes place between people in a small community. Gradually her interests seem to have developed from the general toward the particular, and in the novels that she wrote during the 1940s she analyzes man's romantic nature and his tendency to fall in love with an unobtainable dream. In the novels of the 1950s she becomes more preoccupied with the workings-out of an enduring relationship and turns her attention to the circumstances that cause it to disintegrate. Truly successful relationships are rare in her fiction and suggested rather by a promise of their being so than by their actual attainment. *Catherine Carter* and *The Honours*

Board are the only two novels in which she describes a successful union between her major characters. In general her real gift lies in her ability to analyze pain and loss. *The Humbler Creation* is an example of how well she is able to convey such emotion and relate it to moral necessity. The novels of the 1960s seem to be character- ized by a preoccupation with the problems of good and evil. Iron- ically enough, two of the novels where she is most clearly concerned with the evil in man are ostensibly comic in mode. Her most recent novels are her most assorted since they seem to represent a return to forms and ideas she has tackled before and wishes to approach once more in depth and with maturity. Thus *The Survival of the Fittest* is a mature version of the early panoramic novel; *The Honours Board*, a well-balanced study of the personal relationships in a closed community; and *The Holiday Friend*, an exploration of the indi- vidual's ability to suffer through passion. *The Good Listener* is reminiscent of *The Unspeakable Skipton*, with its cadging hero, and it also indicts the society that permits such people to flourish.

In March 1981 Pamela Hansford Johnson's last novel, *A Bonfire*, was published. Although it is not possible to add a full discussion of it in this book (as it is in press), it is worth noting that it too repre- sents a return to earlier themes. Thus it is set in the period 1924–37, the setting of several novels, notably *The Survival of the Fittest*. Moreover, its protagonist, Emma Sheldrake, has a great deal in com- mon with previous heroines, especially those whose experiences of love and marriage are the subject of chapter seven above. The title, with its reference both to the bonfires of Guy Fawkes night and to the "everlasting bonfire" of Hell, emphasizes more strongly than ever the significance of the burden of guilt so many of Johnson's protagonists suffer from having to bear.

In spite of the seriousness of her commitment Pamela Hansford Johnson's books are never without humor. She writes with irony and compassion and does so with such skill that most situations in her novels are permeated with an ironic vision.

Some of the situations in her novels recur with enough frequency to draw attention to themselves as characteristic. Thus her protag- onists are usually intelligent young men and women from the "middle-middle" class, with literary or artistic ability, whose experience has much in common with her own. She also makes frequent use of a dominant mother and a weak or absent father, and the relationships between mother and child, teacher and pupil are among the most poignantly drawn in her fiction. At the same time she displays an interest in the bizarre and abnormal: nymphomaniacs, homosexuals, old men and women painfully in love with the young, crazed passion, and murder all fall within her range.

In terms of technique Pamela Hansford Johnson has moved away from the experimental toward the traditional. Early in her career as a novelist she favored the form of the psychological novel and made repeated use of counterpoint, stream of consciousness, and interior monolgues. Toward the 1940s, however, she seemed to settle for an objective narrator, and many of her best novels employ this device. Her use of it exploits the perspective that distance and the passing of time lend to an experience, and it is this aspect of her work that most readily comes to mind as evidence of her debt to Marcel Proust.

Since the 1960s she has not made use of an objective narrator and instead has moved over to the method of the great nineteenth-century novelists with an implied third-person narrator and a traditional chronological sequence of events. This technique has enabled her to explore character fully and to comment on the action without seeming to intrude. The increasing sophistication of her use of images and symbols as devices for structural unity is also evident in her mature work. Whereas, in her early fiction, images were evocative and profuse, in her later novels they are chosen with care and usually contribute to the total meaning.

At present the debate about the novel seems to have arrived at a crossroads. After a period of intense experimentation in the 1920s the British novel is generally supposed to have reacted strongly against too much formal experimentation and settled for more traditional techniques.[2] In America, however, innovation in fiction has been highly prized during the 1960s and 1970s, and it is only recently that voices reacting against too much experimentation are being heard.[3] However, at present in Britain, writers like John

Fowles, Malcolm Bradbury, and Christine Brooke-Rose reveal a renewal of interest in experimentation. Pamela Hansford Johnson reflects the pattern of her age in the development of her fiction, with the effects of the experimental period evident in the early novels, and the gradual acceptance of well-tried and tested techniques in the main body of her work. However, in some of her latest novels—for example, *The Unspeakable Skipton, An Error of Judgement,* and *The Good Listener*—there is evidence of a fresh search for new forms to express her particular requirements and a sign that her talent has by no means stagnated or become conventionalized.

Even the novel she was working on at the time of her death and which she intended to call "Adelaide Bartlett," represents a new departure in that it is based on historical material in a way that none of her other novels has been. It is clear that she made a significant contribution to the art of fiction, having written at least a dozen novels that will continue to demand respect.

Notes and References

Preface

1. "Portrait of a Paranoiac," *New Statesman and Nation*, January 10, 1959, p. 48. Hereafter cited as "Paranoiac." This article is incorporated in Walter Allen, *Tradition and Dream* (London, 1964), pp. 257–60.

2. Letter to the author dated February 24, 1975.

Chapter One

1. Pamela Hansford Johnson, *Important to Me, Personalia* (London, 1974), p. 9. Hereafter page references will be to this edition and included in parentheses in the text. The abbreviation *Imp.* will be used when necessary to avoid confusion.

2. "Pamela Hansford Johnson," *Current Biography* (New York, 1948), p. 322. The entry is substantially the same as an article by Helene Scherff Taylor, *Wilson Library Bulletin* 23 (October 1948): 108.

3. Daniel Jones, *My Friend Dylan Thomas* (London, 1977), pp. 34–35.

4. It has not been possible for me to examine this diary because the writing is very faint and the librarian at the Lockwood Memorial Library, State University of New York at Buffalo, says it is impossible to make a copy of it. Extracts from the diary and from Dylan Thomas's letters are quoted at length in Constantine Fitzgibbon, *The Life of Dylan Thomas* (London, 1965), pp. 126–60. Several of Dylan Thomas's letters to Pamela Hansford Johnson are printed in full in Constantine Fitzgibbon, *Selected Letters of Dylan Thomas* (London, 1966). An account of the relationship between Pamela Hansford Johnson and Dylan Thomas is also given in Paul Ferris's recent biography, *Dylan*

Thomas (London, 1977), pp. 100–27. Pamela Hansford Johnson's own account appears in *Imp.*, pp. 140–49.

5. See, for example, "Is the Novel in Decline?" *Books of Today* 2 (May 1947): 2, and "The Sick-room Hush over the English Novel," *The Listener*, August 11, 1949, p. 236.

6. In an interview with the author August 1975. C. P. Snow died on July 1, 1980.

7. "A Corvo of Our Day," *Times Literary Supplement*, January 9, 1959, p .18. Hereafter cited as "Corvo." John Raymond, *The Doge of Dover* (London, 1960), contains the same essay.

8. *Newsweek*, May 27, 1968, p. 61.

9. See, for example, *Imp.*, p. 242.

10. *Listener*, August 11, 1949, p. 235.

Chapter Two

1. Pamela Hansford Johnson, *This Bed Thy Centre*, 2nd ed. (London, 1962), preface, p. 6. Hereafter page references will be to this edition and included in parentheses in the text. The abbreviation *Bed* will be used when necessary to avoid confusion.

2. *Pamela Hansford Johnson* (London, 1968), p. 14.

3. Pamela Hansford Johnson, *Here Today* (London, 1937), p. 361. Hereafter page references will be to this edition and included in parentheses in the text.

4. *John O'London's Weekly*, April 20, 1935, p. 88.

5. *New Statesman and Nation*, April 13, 1935, p. 525.

6. *New York Times Book Review*, September 15, 1935, p. 7.

7. Ibid.

8. *The Psychological Novel 1900–1950* (New York, 1955), p. 16.

9. *New Republic*, November 20, 1935, p. 140.

Chapter Three

1. *Times Literary Supplement*, September 25, 1937, p. 693.

2. *New York Times Book Review*, February 27, 1938, p. 6.

3. Pamela Hansford Johnson, *The Monument* (London, 1938), p. 418. Hereafter page references will be to this edition and included in parentheses in the text.

4. Pamela Hansford Johnson, *The Survival of the Fittest* (London,

1968), p. 48. Hereafter page references will be to this edition and included in parentheses in the text.

5. *Nation*, August 19, 1968, p. 125.

6. *New York Times Book Review*, July 7, 1968, p. 22.

Chapter Four

1. Pamela Hansford Johnson, *Girdle of Venus* (London, 1939), p. 196. Hereafter page references will be to this edition and included in parentheses in the text.

2. Pamela Hansford Johnson, *The Family Pattern* (London, 1942), p. 143. Hereafter page references will be to this edition and included in parentheses in the text.

3. V. V. Ivasheva, "Tvorcheskii Put, P. Khensford Dzhonson," *Vestnik Moskovkogo Universiteta Filologia* 1 (Moscow, 1968): 20 ("The works of P. Hansford Johnson"). Includes a report of an interview with the author in 1965.

Chapter Five

1. Pamela Hansford Johnson, *Avenue of Stone*, 2nd ed. (London, 1973), preface, p. 5. Note that page references to the quotations from *An Avenue of Stone* that are included in parentheses in the text are to the 1st ed. (London, 1947). The preface is only in the 2nd ed. See also the preface to *Too Dear for My Possessing*, 2nd ed. (London, 1972), p. 7. Hereafter page references will be to this edition and included in parentheses in the text.

2. Pamela Hansford Johnson, *Winter Quarters* (London, 1943), p. 4. Hereafter page references will be to this edition and will be included in parentheses in the text.

3. *New York Times Book Review*, June 18, 1944, p. 6.

4. These three critics are John Hampson, *Spectator*, February 11, 1944, p. 132; William Poster, *New York Herald Tribune Weekly Book Review*, June 18, 1944, p. 6; and James Stern, *Nation*, July 29, 1944, p. 135.

5. Isabel Quigly, "Pamela Hansford Johnson," *Contemporary Novelists*, eds. James Vinson and A. L. Kirkpatrick, 2nd ed. (London and New York, 1976), p. 725.

6. Isabel Quigly, *Pamela Hansford Johnson* (London, 1968), p. 17.

7. *New York Times Book Review*, July 28, 1940, p. 7.

8. "Corvo," p. 18.

9. *Times Literary Supplement*, May 2, 1975, p. 473.

10. Quigly, *Johnson*, p. 18.

11. "Corvo," p. 18.

12. Ibid.

13. Pamela Hansford Johnson, *A Summer to Decide*, 2nd ed. (London, 1948), p. 95. Hereafter page references will be to this edition and included in parentheses in the text.

14. *New York Herald Tribune Weekly Book Review*, July 28, 1940, p. 2.

15. *New Republic*, September 2, 1940, p. 307.

16. "Elegiac Saga," *New Statesman*, May 17, 1968, p. 655. Hereafter cited as "Elegiac."

17. Janet Adam Smith, *Spectator*, August 23, 1940, p. 202, and Desmond Hawkins, *New Statesman and Nation*, August 31, 1940, p. 214.

Chapter Six

1. *New York Times Book Review*, March 1, 1936, p. 7.

2. Pamela Hansford Johnson, *Blessed Above Women* (London, 1936), p. 122. Hereafter page references will be to this edition and included in parentheses in the text.

3. *New York Times Book Review*, March 1, 1936, p. 7.

4. *New York Times Book Review*, July 1, 1945, p. 15.

5. Ibid.

6. Pamela Hansford Johnson, *The Trojan Brothers* (London, 1944), p. 17. Hereafter page references will be to this edition and included in parentheses in the text.

7. See, for example, *Manchester Guardian*, October 20, 1944, p. 3; *New Statesman and Nation*, November 18, 1944, p. 28; and *New York Herald Tribune Weekly Book Review*, June 24, 1945, p. 6.

8. Pamela Hansford Johnson, *The Holiday Friend* (London, 1972), p. 123. Hereafter page references will be to this edition and included in parentheses in the text.

9. *New Yorker*, April 28, 1973, p. 19.

10. *Times Literary Supplement*, October 27, 1972, p. 1274.

Chapter Seven

1. Byatt, "Elegiac," p. 655.
2. Allen, "Paranoiac," p. 48.
3. Pamela Hansford Johnson, *The Philistines* (London, 1949), p. 13. Hereafter page references will be to this edition and included in parentheses in the text.
4. *Times Literary Supplement*, October 21, 1949, p. 677.
5. Pamela Hansford Johnson, *Catherine Carter* (London, 1968), p. 7. Hereafter page references will be to this edition and included in parentheses in the text.
6. Allen, "Paranoiac," p. 48.
7. *New York Times Book Review*, March 27, 1955, p. 5.
8. *Imp.*, p. 202.
9. Pamela Hansford Johnson, *An Impossible Marriage* (London, 1954), p. 1. Hereafter page references will be to this edition and be included in parentheses in the text.
10. Byatt, "Elegiac," p. 654.
11. *New Republic*, September 2, 1940, p. 307.

Chapter Eight

1. Susan Black, *New Republic*, March 21, 1960, p. 19.
2. Allen, "Paranoiac," p. 48.
3. John Gardner, *On Moral Fiction* (New York, 1977). See especially Chapter 2, pp. 18–40 passim.
4. *New York Times Book Review*, February 28, 1960, p. 4.
5. Pamela Hansford Johnson, *The Last Resort* (London, 1965), p. 78. Hereafter page references will be to this edition and included in parentheses in the text.
6. *New York Times Book Review*, February 24, 1957, p. 4.
7. Byatt, "Elegiac," p. 655.
8. Allen, "Paranoiac," p. 48.
9. Pamela Hansford Johnson, *The Humbler Creation* (London, 1959), p. 13. Hereafter page references will be to this edition and included in parentheses in the text.
10. *Spectator*, September 25, 1959, p. 416.
11. *Saturday Review*, March 5, 1960, p. 15.
12. *New Republic*, March 21, 1960, p. 19.

13. *Times Literary Supplement*, September 25, 1959, p. 541.

Chapter Nine

1. *Contemporary Novelists* (London, 1977), p. 686.
2. "Corvo," p. 18.
3. *Saturday Review*, July 20, 1963, p. 22.
4. Allen, "Paranoiac," p. 48.
5. Pamela Hansford Johnson, *The Unspeakable Skipton* (London, 1959), p. vii. Hereafter page references will be to this edition and included in parentheses in the text.
6. *Times Literary Supplement*, January 14, 1977, p. 27.
7. "Corvo," p. 18.
8. Pamela Hansford Johnson, *Cork Street, Next to the Hatter's: A Novel in Bad Taste* (London, 1965), p. 67. Hereafter page references will be to this edition and included in parentheses in the text.
9. "Corvo," p. 18.
10. *New York Herald Tribune Weekly Book Review*, February 8, 1959, p. 6.
11. Bernard Shaw, *Sixteen Self Sketches* (London, 1949), p. 54.
12. *Time*, July 26, 1963, p. 56.
13. Pamela Hansford Johnson, *Night and Silence, Who Is Here? An American Comedy* (London, 1968), Penguin Books, p. 165. Hereafter page references will be to this edition and included in parentheses in the text (it has not been possible to obtain any other edition in Sweden).
14. Pamela Hansford Johnson, *On Iniquity: Some Personal Reflections Arising Out of the Moors Murder Trial* (London, 1967), p. 37. In "The World of Books" program broadcast on the British Broadcasting Service on October 9, 1965, Pamela Hansford Johnson discusses Cork Street at some length with T. G. Rosenthal. Among other things she says, "But if you write a play which is really based on cruelty and violence, pure and simple, then you are living [*sic*] out the other important things of life and you are writing what I think is not only very shallow, but ultimately very corrupting. I think it's very bad for art. That is, you're writing an art which tends only to excite. If you write an art which tends to excite then the sort of theatre of ideas I mean just flies away."
15. In "The World of Books" broadcast (see note 14) Pamela Hans-

ford Johnson endorses this interpretation: "I mean the novel is—er—possibly my bad taste. I mean have it your own way. I don't care. But what I meant was that Tom Hariot went to a play that everybody likes very very much indeed, and he thinks it's perfectly appalling you see. I mean his taste is bad against the current of the time, which as I say is a very conformist current."

16. *Saturday Review*, October 9, 1965, p. 49.

17. In an interview with the author (August 1975).

Chapter Ten

1. Pamela Hansford Johnson, *An Error of Judgement* (London, 1962), p. 9. Hereafter page references will be to this edition and included in parentheses in the text.

2. *Yale Review*, Winter 1963, pp. 261–62.

3. *New York Times Book Review*, September 16, 1962, p. 5.

4. Pamela Hansford Johnson, *The Honours Board* (London, 1970), p. 24.

5. *New Statesman*, August 14, 1970, p. 185.

6. *New York Times Book Review*, September 20, 1970, p. 42.

7. Pamela Hansford Johnson, *The Good Listener* (London, 1975), p. 237. Hereafter page references will be to this edition and included in parentheses in the text.

8. Pamela Hansford Johnson, *The Good Husband* (London, 1978), p. 164. Hereafter page references will be to this edition and included in parentheses in the text.

9. *Times Literary Supplement*, June 20, 1975, p. 689, and *New York Times Book Review*, September 28, 1975, p. 30.

10. *Times Literary Supplement*, June 20, 1975, p. 689.

11. *New Statesman*, October 27, 1978, p. 555.

12. *Times Literary Supplement*, November 3, 1978, p. 1277.

Chapter Eleven

1. "Against Dryness: A Polemical Sketch," *The Novel Today*, ed. Malcolm Bradbury (London, 1977), p. 23.

2. Several writers, notably American, have propounded this theory. See, for example, Frederick R. Karl, *A Reader's Guide to the Contemporary English Novel* (London, 1961, rev. 1972); James Gindin, *Postwar British Fiction: New Accents and Attitudes* (Berkeley, Calif., 1962);

and Rubin Rabinovitz, *The Reaction against Experiment in the English Novel: 1950–1960* (New York, 1967).

3. One of the most influential is that of the novelist John Gardner. See, for example, *On Moral Fiction* (New York, 1977).

Selected Bibliography

PRIMARY SOURCES

1. Novels

This Bed Thy Centre. London: Chapman and Hall; New York: Harcourt Brace, 1935. Reissued with a Preface, London: Macmillan, 1961.

Blessed Above Women. London: Chapman and Hall; New York: Harcourt Brace, 1936.

Here Today. London: Chapman and Hall, 1937.

World's End. London: Chapman and Hall, 1937; New York: Carrick and Evans, 1938.

The Monument. London: Chapman and Hall; New York: Carrick and Evans, 1938.

Girdle of Venus. London: Chapman and Hall, 1939.

Too Dear for My Possessing. London: Collins; New York: Carrick and Evans, 1940. Reissued with a Preface, London: Macmillan, 1972; Penguin Books, 1976.

Tidy Death, with Neil Stewart (as Nap Lombard). London: Cassel, 1940.

The Family Pattern. London: Collins, 1942.

Winter Quarters. London: Collins, 1943; New York: Macmillan, 1944.

Murder's a Swine, with Neil Stewart (as Nap Lombard). London: Hutchinson, 1943; as *The Grinning Pig*, New York: Simon and Schuster, 1943.

The Trojan Brothers. London: Joseph, 1944; New York: Macmillan, 1945.

An Avenue of Stone. London: Joseph, 1947; New York: Macmillan,

1948; Penguin Books, 1953. Reissued with a Preface, London: Macmillan, 1973.

A Summer to Decide. London: Joseph, 1948; Penguin Books, 1954, New York: Scribner, 1975. Reissued with a Preface, London: Macmillan, 1975.

The Philistines. London: Joseph, 1949.

Catherine Carter. London: Macmillan; New York: Knopf, 1952; Pan Books, 1957; London: Macmillan, 1968.

An Impossible Marriage. London: Macmillan; New York: Harcourt Brace, 1954.

The Last Resort. London: Macmillan, 1956. As *The Sea and the Wedding.* New York: Harcourt Brace, 1957; London: Macmillan, 1965.

The Humbler Creation. London: Macmillan, 1959; New York: Harcourt Brace, 1960, Penguin Books, 1961.

The Unspeakable Skipton. London: Macmillan; New York: Harcourt Brace, 1959; Penguin Books, 1961; New York: Scribner, 1981.

An Error of Judgement. London: Macmillan; New York: Harcourt Brace, 1962; Penguin Books, 1965.

Night and Silence, Who Is Here? An American Comedy. London: Macmillan; New York: Scribner, 1963; Penguin Books, 1968.

Cork Street, Next to the Hatter's: A Novel in Bad Taste. London: Macmillan; New York: Scribner, 1965.

The Survival of the Fittest. London: Macmillan; New York: Scribner, 1968.

The Honours Board. London: Macmillan; New York: Scribner, 1970.

The Holiday Friend. London: Macmillan, 1972; New York: Scribner, 1973; Penguin Books, 1977.

The Good Listener. London: Macmillan; New York: Scribner, 1975; London: Prior, 1976.

The Good Husband. London: Macmillan; New York: Scribner, 1978.

A Bonfire. London: Macmillan; New York: Scribner, 1981.

2. Uncollected Short Stories

"Ghost of Honour," *John O'London's Weekly,* December 7, 1935, p. 377.

"The Hero," *John O'London's Weekly,* March 28, 1936, p. 997.

"Judas and the Jug," *John O'London's Weekly*, April 18, 1936, p. 77.

"The Traveller," *John O'London's Weekly*, October 30, 1936, p. 193.

"Sanctuary," in *English Review* (London), February 1937, pp. 238–42.

"Altarwise by Owl-light," *English Review* (London), pp. 718–32.

"Look at Your Uncle Jim," *John O'London's Weekly*, June 25, 1937, pp. 489–90.

"Cedric," *John O'London's Weekly*, April 29, 1938, pp. 145–46.

"A Song Saved His Life," *John O'London's Weekly*, December 2, 1938, p. 387.

"Sweethearts," *John O'London's Weekly*, December 2, 1938, pp. 359–60.

"Scrap-book for 1938," *Spectator* (London), December 16, 1938.

"My Books Are My Children," *Winter's Tales 1*. London: Macmillan, 1955.

"Death of a Duchess," *Winter's Tales 3*. London: Macmillan, 1957.

3. Plays

Corinth House (produced London, 1948). London: Macmillan; New York: St. Martin's Press, 1954.

The Supper Dance, with C. P. Snow. London: Evans, 1951.

Family Party, with C. P. Snow. London: Evans, 1951.

Spare the Rod, with C. P. Snow. London: Evans, 1951.

To Murder Mrs. Mortimer, with C. P. Snow. London: Evans, 1951.

The Pigeon with the Silver Foot, with C. P. Snow. London: Evans, 1951.

Her Best Foot Forward, with C. P. Snow. London: Evans, 1951.

Six Proust Reconstructions (broadcast, 1948–56). London: Macmillan, 1958; as *Proust Recaptured: Six Radio Sketches, Based on the Author's Characters*, Chicago: University of Chicago Press, 1958.

The Rehearsal, with Kitty Black, adaptation of a play by Jean Anouilh (produced London, 1961; New York, 1963). London: Methuen, 1961; New York, Coward McCann, 1962.

The Public Prosecutor, with C. P. Snow, adaptation of a play by Georgi Dzhagarov, translated by Marguerite Alexieva (produced London, 1967). London: Peter Owen, 1969.

Radio Plays: Six Proust Reconstructions: *The Duchess at Sunset*, 1948; *Swann in Love*, 1952; *Madame de Charlus*, 1954; *Albertine Regained*, 1954; *Saint-Loup*, 1955; and *A Window at Montjaurain*, 1956.

4. Verse

Symphony for Full Orchestra. London: Sunday Referee–Parton, 1934.

5. Nonfiction, Books

Thomas Wolfe: A Critical Study. London: Heinemann, 1947. As
   Hungry Gulliver: An English Critical Appraisal of Thomas Wolfe.
   New York: Scribner, 1948.
Ivy Compton-Burnett. London: Longman, 1953.
*On Iniquity: Some Personal Reflections Arising Out of the Moors
   Murder Trial*. London: Macmillan; New York: Scribner, 1967.
Important to Me: Personalia. London: Macmillan, 1974; New York:
   Scribner, 1975.

6. Nonfiction, Miscellaneous

"Scrap-Book for 1938," *Spectator*, December 16, 1938, pp. 1043–44.
"What I Cannot Bear About Novels," *Books of Today* 1 (September
   1946): 1–2.
"Is the Novel in Decline?," *Books of Today* 2 (May 1947): 1–2.
"A Question of Taste," *Books of Today* 3 (January 1948): 1–2.
"Unpleasant Characters," *Books of Today* 4 (June 1949): 1–2.
"The Sick-room Hush over the English Novel," *Listener*, August 11,
   1949, pp. 235–36.
"Three Novelists and the Drawing of Character; C. P. Snow, Joyce
   Cary and Ivy Compton-Burnett," *Essays and Studies*, 3. London:
   John Murray, 1950.
"On the Future of Prose-Drama," *Corinth House*. London: Evans, 1950,
   pp. 3–53.
"Books and Writers," *Spectator*, May 18, 1951, p. 657.
Introduction to A. Trollope, *Barchester Towers*. London: Collins, 1952.
"Seventeen Further Memoirs," *Adam International Review*, ed. Miron
   Grindea (Dylan Thomas Memorial Number) 21, 1953.
"Looking at Pictures," *Spectator*, January 15, 1954, pp. 72–73.
"Looking at Words," *Spectator*, April 2, 1954, pp. 393–94.
"Looking at Arithmetic," *Spectator*, May 28, 1954, pp. 651–52.
"The Novel of Marcel Proust," *Marcel Proust's Letters to His Mother*,
   ed. G. D. Painter. London: Rider, 1956, pp. 11–31.
Review of Doris Lessing's *The Habit of Loving*, *New Statesman*, No-
   vember 23, 1957, p. 700.

"The Debate about the Novel," *New Statesman*, August 9, 1958, pp. 172–73.

"Christine Longford's Making Conversation," *Times Literary Supplement*, November 28, 1968, pp. 1332–33.

"Thomas Wolfe and the Kicking Season," *Encounter* 12 (April 1959): 77–80.

"Modern Fiction and the English Understatement," *Times Literary Supplement* (Special Autumn Number), August 7, 1959, p. iii.

"Secret of Bruges," *Vogue*, Boulder, Colorado, September 1, 1959, p. 64.

"Proust at Full-Length," *New Statesman*, September 19, 1959, pp. 361–62.

"Most Remarkable Walk in London," *Vogue*, October 1, 1961, p. 145.

"If She Writes, Must She Be a Lady?" *New York Times Book Review*, December 31, 1961, pp. 1, 22.

"The Goncourts," *New Statesman*, June 15, 1962, p. 870.

"Special Pleasure of Praise from the Surly," *Vogue*, October 1, 1962, pp. 192–93.

"Marcel Proust: Illusion and Reality," *Royal Society of Literature: Essays by Diverse Hands*, 32. Oxford: Univ. Press, 1963, pp. 58–71.

"Belgium," *Mademoiselle* (Boulder, Colorado), January 1964, p. 58.

"Compulsory Sex Scene," *Vogue*, January 1, 1965, p. 134ff.

"Speaking of Books: Anthony Trollope, an Odd Fish," *New York Times Book Review*, April 25, 1965, p. 2.

"Ghastly Transcripts," *Life*, New York, August 12, 1966, pp. 61–62.

"Letter from Abroad: A Test of Our Times," *McCall's*, December 1966, p. 28.

"Speaking Out: We Need More Censorship," *Saturday Evening Post*, January 14, 1967, p. 240.

"The Man Who Knew Shakespeare," *Holiday*, November 1967, p. 34.

"Speaking of Books: The Forsythe Saga," *New York Times Book Review*, March 12, 1967, p. 2.

"The Sexual Life in Dickens's Novels," *Dickens 1970: Centenary Essays*, ed. M. Slater. London: Chapman, 1970, pp. 173–94.

"Peddling the Pornography of Violence," *Encounter* 34 (February 1970): 70–76.

"Triumph over Time," *Marcel Proust 1871–1922: A Centenary Volume*, ed. Peter Quenell. London: Weidenfeld and Nicolson, 1971, pp. 195–205.

"The Papal Paranoiac," Review of Miriam J. Benkovitz, *Frederick Rolfe: Baron Corvo*, in the *Times Literary Supplement*, January 14, 1977, p. 27.

7. Manuscript Collection: University of Texas, Austin

Dylan Thomas Correspondence and Pamela Hansford Johnson's Diaries: Lockwood Memorial Library, State University of New York at Buffalo.

SECONDARY SOURCES

1. Book Reviews

Book reviews selected for their comparative importance and length and listed under the titles of Pamela Hansford Johnson's novels in chronological order. Four novels, *Here Today*, *Girdle of Venus*, *The Family Pattern*, and *The Philistines*, are not mentioned in *Book Review Digest*. *A Bonfire* was published while this book was in press.

This Bed Thy Centre

BELL, LISLE, *New York Herald Tribune Books*, September 15, 1935, p. 15.
CHURCH, RICHARD. *John O'London's Weekly*, April 20, 1935, p. 88.
CONNOLLY, CYRIL. *New Statesman and Nation*, April 13, 1935, p. 525.
New Republic, November 20, 1935, p. 56.
O'FAOLAIN, SEAN. *Spectator*, April 19, 1935, p. 668.
SOUTHRON, JANE SPENCE. *New York Times Book Review*, September 15, 1935, p. 7.
Times Literary Supplement (London), April 25, 1935, p. 273.

Blessed Above Women

CONNOLLY, CYRIL. *New Statesman and Nation*, February 1, 1936, p. 11.
CONRAD, GEORGE. *New York Herald Tribune Books*, March 1, 1936, p. 12.

John O'London's Weekly, January 25, 1936, p. 665.
Manchester Guardian, February 14, 1936, p. 7.
New York Times Book Review, March 1, 1936, p. 7.
Saturday Review, July 11, 1936, p. 18.

World's End

GIBSON, WILFRID. *Manchester Guardian*, September 21, 1937, p. 7.
O'BRIEN, KATE. *Spectator*, December 24, 1937, p. 1156.
O'FAOLAIN, SEAN. *John O'London's Weekly*, September 24, 1937, p. 944.
ROSS, MARY. *New York Herald Tribune Books*, February 27, 1938, p. 6.
Saturday Review, March 12, 1938, p. 20.
SHAWE-TAYLOR, DESMOND. *New Statesman and Nation*, October 9, 1937, p. 567.
Times Literary Supplement, September 25, 1937, p. 693.
WALTON, EDITH H. *New York Times Book Review*, February 27, 1938, p. 6.

The Monument

MERTON, J. K. *Commonweal*, October 21, 1938, p. 680.
ROSS, MARY. *New York Herald Tribune Books*, September 18, 1938, p. 12.
SOUTHRON, JANE SPENCE. *New York Times Book Review*, September 11, 1938, p. 7.

Too Dear For My Possessing

BELL, LISLE. *New York Herald Tribune Books*, July 28, 1940, p. 2.
HAUSER, MARIANNE. *New Republic*, September 2, 1940, p. 307.
HAWKINS, DESMOND. *New Statesman and Nation*, August 31, 1940, p. 214.
Saturday Review of Literature, August 3, 1940, p. 21.
SMITH, JANET ADAM. *Spectator*, August 23, 1940, p. 202.
SOUTHRON, JANE SPENCE. *New York Times Book Review*, July 28, 1940, p. 7.
Times Literary Supplement, August 31, 1940, p. 421.

Winter Quarters

HAMPSON, JOHN. *Spectator*, February 11, 1944, p. 132.
MALLET, ISABELLE. *New York Times Book Review*, June 18, 1940, p. 6.
POSTER, WILLIAM. *New Republic*, July 17, 1944, p. 82.
————. *Herald Tribune Book Review*, June 18, 1944, p. 6.
STERN, JAMES. *Nation*, July 29, 1944, p. 135.
Times Literary Supplement, December 25, 1943, p. 623.

The Trojan Brothers

Christian Science Monitor, June 23, 1945, p. 14.
CONRAD, GEORGE. *Herald Tribune Weekly Book Review*, June 24, 1945, p. 6.
MARTIN, JANE. *New York Times Book Review*, July 1, 1945, p. 15.
POPE-HENNESSY, UNA. *New Statesman and Nation*, November 18, 1944.
ROBERTS, R. E. *Saturday Review of Literature*, June 16, 1945, p. 28.
Times Literary Supplement, November 11, 1944, p. 551.

An Avenue of Stone

ROSS, MARY. *New York Herald Tribune Weekly Book Review*, March 14, 1948, p. 6.
SAVAGE, D. S. *Spectator*, May 30, 1947, p. 632.
Times Literary Supplement, May 31, 1947, p. 265.

A Summer to Decide (not included in Book Review Digest when first published but included in 1976 after reissue)

DUCHENE, ANNE. *Times Literary Supplement*, May 2, 1975, p. 473.

Catherine Carter

CHARQUES, R. D. *Spectator*, January 25, 1952, p. 122.
KELLY, JAMES. *New York Times Book Review*, July 20, 1952, p. 5.
McLAUGHLIN, RICHARD. *Theatre Arts*, August 1952, p. 13.
RAYMOND, JOHN. *New Statesman and Nation*, February 2, 1952, p. 133.
ROSS, MARY. *New York Herald Tribune Book Review*, July 20, 1952, p. 5.

SMITH, HARRISON. *Saturday Review of Literature*, July 19, 1952,
   p. 14.
Times Literary Supplement, February 1, 1952, p. 89.

An Impossible Marriage

METCALF, JOHN. *Spectator*, April 2, 1954, p. 416.
NERBER, JOHN. *New York Times Book Review*, March 27, 1955,
   p. 5.
ROMILLY, GILES. *New Statesman and Nation*, April 3, 1954, p. 445.
Times Literary Supplement, April 2, 1954, p. 212.
WEBSTER, H. C. *Saturday Review of Literature*, April 9, 1955, p. 19.

The Last Resort (American title, *The Sea and the Wedding*)

JANEWAY, ELIZABETH. *New York Times Book Review*, March 3,
   1957, p. 4.
New Yorker, March 23, 1957, p. 16.
SMITH, HARRISON. *Saturday Review of Literature*, March 9, 1957,
   p. 16.
Times Literary Supplement, November 16, 1956, p. 677.
TUNSTALL, CAROLINE. *New York Herald Tribune Book Review*,
   March 3, 1957, p. 4.

The Humbler Creation

BLACK, SUSAN M. *New Republic*, March 21, 1960, p. 19.
COLEMAN, JOHN. *Spectator*, September 25, 1959, p. 416.
HICKS, GRANVILLE. *Saturday Review of Literature*, March 5, 1960,
   p. 15.
NAIPUL, V. S. *New Statesman*, September 26, 1959, p. 401.
SYKES, GERALD. *New York Times Book Review*, February 28, 1960,
   p. 4.
Times Literary Supplement, September 25, 1959, p. 541.
TUNSTALL, CAROLINE. *New York Herald Tribune Book Review*,
   February 28, 1960, p. 6.

The Unspeakable Skipton

ALLEN, WALTER. *New Statesman*, January 10, 1959, p. 48.
BACON, MARTHA. *Saturday Review of Literature*, January 24, 1959,
   p. 31.

BALLIETT, WHITNEY. *New Yorker*, March 21, 1959, p. 167.
BECKET, ROGER. *New York Herald Tribune Book Review*, February 8, 1959, p. 6.
CURLEY, T. F. *Commonweal*, February 20, 1959, p. 549.
KERMODE, FRANK. *Spectator*, January 9, 1959, p. 54.
PIPPETT, AILEEN. *New York Times Book Review*, January 25, 1959, p. 6.
Time, February 16, 1959, p. 106.
Times Literary Supplement, "A Corvo of Our Day," January 9, 1959, p. 18.

An Error of Judgement

CORKE, HILARY. *New Republic*, October 27, 1962, p. 27.
DANIEL, JOHN. *Spectator*, July 20, 1962, p. 94.
PRICE, MARTIN. *Yale Review*, Winter 1963, p. 261.
SYKES, GERALD. *New York Times Book Review*, September 16, 1962, p. 5.
Times Literary Supplement, July 20, 1962, p. 521.

Night and Silence, Who Is Here?

BAKER, CARLOS. *New York Times Book Review*, July 28, 1963, p. 4.
Christian Science Monitor, July 25, 1963, p. 7.
GAVIN, W. F. *America*, July 27, 1963, p. 102.
HICKS, GRANVILLE. *Saturday Review of Literature*, July 20, 1963, p. 21.
LAMPORT, FELICIA. *New York Herald Tribune Book Review*, July 21, 1963, p. 8.
MILLER, KARL. *New Statesman*, June 14, 1963, p. 909.
Time, July 26, 1963, p. 83.
Times Literary Supplement, May 31, 1963, p. 385.

Cork Street, Next to the Hatter's: A Novel in Bad Taste

CROMBIE, JOHN. *Christian Science Monitor*, October 14, 1965, p. 10.
GAVIN, W. F. *America*, November 6, 1965, p. 540.
HICKS, GRANVILLE. *Saturday Review of Literature*, October 9, 1965, p. 49.
LAFORE, LAURENCE. *New York Times Book Review*, November 14, 1965, p. 61.

MAYNE, RICHARD. *New Statesman*, October 1, 1965, p. 489.
Times Literary Supplement, September 30, 1965, p. 850.
WEEKS, EDWARD. *Atlantic*, November 1965, p. 182.

The Survival of the Fittest

BYATT, A. S. *New Statesman*, "Elegiac Saga," May 17, 1968, pp. 654–55.
CHARLES, GERDA, *Nation*, August 9, 1968, p. 124.
DAVIS, R. G. *New York Times Book Review*, July 7, 1968, p. 22.
HALL, JAMES. *Saturday Review of Literature*, August 3, 1968, p. 24.
MADDOCKS, MELVIN. *Christian Science Monitor*, May 23, 1968, p. 7.
Newsweek, May 27, 1968, p. 97.
Times Literary Supplement, May 16, 1968, p. 497.
WEEKS, EDWARD. *Atlantic*, July 1968, p. 101.

The Honours Board

KNOWLES, JOHN. *New York Times Book Review*, September 20, 1970, p. 4.
PARKER, D. L. *Christian Science Monitor*, October 22, 1970, p. 8.
TREVOR, WILLIAM. *New Statesman*, August 14, 1970, p. 80.

The Holiday Friend

New Yorker, April 28, 1973, p. 19.
Times Literary Supplement, October 27, 1973, p. 1274.

The Good Listener

ABEEL, ERICA. *New York Times Book Review*, September 28, 1975, p. 30.
BARNES, JULIAN. *New Statesman*, July 4, 1975, p. 30.
DUCHENE, ANNE. *Times Literary Supplement*, June 20, 1975, p. 689.

The Good Husband

BOYD, WILLIAM. *New Statesman*, October 27, 1978, p. 555.
DUCHENE, ANNE. *Times Literary Supplement*, November 3, 1978, p. 1277.

2. Books and articles dealing with Pamela Hansford Johnson's life and/or work.

ALLEN, WALTER. *Tradition and Dream*. London: Phoenix, 1964, pp. 257–60. This section is substantially the same as the article "Portrait of a Paranoiac," *New Statesman*, January 10, 1959, p. 48. Primarily a discussion of *The Unspeakable Skipton* but mentions *The Last Resort*.

ALLSOP, KENNETH. "Iniquity?" *Encounter* 29, (July 1967): 62.

BALASHEV, P. *Afterword to Russian Translation of "The Decisive Summer."* Moscow: Progress, 1969.

BOROWITZ, A. "The Snows on the Moors: C. P. Snow and Pamela Hansford Johnson," *Innocence and Arsenic, Studies in Crime and Literature*. New York: Harper, 1977.

BRODIE, JOHN. "First Impressions of Literary People," *Books of Today*, July 1947, p. 5.

BURGESS, ANTHONY. *The Novel Now*, 2nd ed. London: Faber, 1971, pp. 67–69. Brief discussion especially of *The Unspeakable Skipton*.

FERRIS, PAUL. *Dylan Thomas*. London: Hodder, 1977. Contains a section dealing with the relationship between Dylan Thomas and P. Hansford Johnson.

FITZGIBBON, CONSTANTINE. *The Life of Dylan Thomas*. London: Dent, 1965. Contains a section dealing with the relationship between Dylan Thomas and Pamela Hansford Johnson with extracts from his letters to her and from her diary.

————. *Selected Letters of Dylan Thomas*. London: Dent, 1966. Contains full text of several letters from Dylan Thomas to P. Hansford Johnson.

IVASHEVA, V. V., "Tvorcheskii Put, P. Khensford Dzhonson" (The works of P. Hansford Johnson), *Vestnik Moskovskogo Universiteta Filologia* 1 (Moscow, 1968).

JONES, DANIEL. *My Friend Dylan Thomas*. London: Dent, 1977. Contains an account of his meeting with P. Hansford Johnson and V. Neuberg's circle of poets.

KARL, F. R. *A Reader's Guide to the Contemporary English Novel*, 2nd ed. London: Thames and Hudson, 1972.

New Yorker, "Chubb Fellow" 37:44 (December 16, 1961).

Newsweek, "Portrait" 40, (July 21, 1952): 91.

QUIGLY, ISABEL. *Contemporary Novelists*. Eds. James Vinson and

D. L. Kirkpatrick. 2nd ed. London and New York: St. James/St. Martin's, 1977. Contains a select bibliography and a survey of P. Hansford Johnson's work.

————. *Pamela Hansford Johnson*, Writers and Their Work Series. London: Longmans, 1968. Brochure published for the British Council and the National Book League. The only longer study that exists of P. Hansford Johnson's work.

RAYMOND, JOHN. "A Corvo of Our Day," *The Doge of Dover*. London: MacGibbon, 1960. This article was first published in *The Times Literary Supplement*, January 9, 1959, and gives an excellent brief survey of P. Hansford Johnson's most important work up to and including *The Unspeakable Skipton*.

Saturday Review of Literature. "Portrait" 38 (April 9, 1955): 19.

————. "Portrait" 40 (March 9, 1957): 16.

Twentieth Century Authors: A Biographical Dictionary of Modern Literature, First Supp. Eds. Stanley J. Kunitz and V. Colby. New York: Wilson, 1955, pp. 496–97.

Vogue. "Sir Charles and Lady Snow" (Boulder, Colorado), March 1, 1961.

Index